The Art and Science of Natural Dyes

PRINCIPLES, EXPERIMENTS, AND RESULTS

Joy Boutrup | Catharine Ellis

Schiffer Publishing Ltd

4880 Lower Valley Road • Atglen, PA 19310

Other Schiffer Books on Related Subjects:

Dimensional Cloth: Sculpture by Contemporary Textile Artists, Andra F. Stanton, foreword by Josephine Stealey, ISBN 978-0-7643-5536-3

Master Your Craft: Strategies for Designing, Making, and Selling Artisan Work, Tien Chiu, foreword by Christopher H. Amundsen, ISBN 978-0-7643-5145-7

Linen: From Flax Seed to Woven Cloth, Linda Heinrich, ISBN 978-0-7643-3466-5

Designed by Danielle D. Farmer
Cover design by Brenda McCallum
Diagrams and drawings by Joy Boutrup
Dyed samples by Catharine Ellis, with the exception of woven and painted textile on p. 95 by Bethanne Knudson

Type set in MaribelSuit/Zurich

ISBN: 978-0-7643-5633-9
Printed in China

Published by Schiffer Publishing, Ltd.
4880 Lower Valley Road
Atglen, PA 19310
Phone: (610) 593-1777; Fax: (610) 593-2002
E-mail: Info@schifferbooks.com
Web: www.schifferbooks.com

For our complete selection of fine books on this and related subjects, please visit our website at www.schifferbooks.com. You may also write for a free catalog.

Schiffer Publishing's titles are available at special discounts for bulk purchases for sales promotions or premiums. Special editions, including personalized covers, corporate imprints, and excerpts, can be created in large quantities for special needs. For more information, contact the publisher.

We are always looking for people to write books on new and related subjects. If you have an idea for a book, please contact us at proposals@schifferbooks.com

We would like to dedicate this book

to our friend and mentor, Michel Garcia. His enthusiasm for natural dyeing has inspired a new generation of natural dyers. Michel has connected history and science with the art of dyeing and has introduced old practices with sustainable applications. Without his pioneering work, creative exploration, and generosity, we would not have come together to write this book.

Contents

Contents

Foreword
Yoshiko Iwamoto Wada

For millennia, humans perceived color through nature and its reflections in human interpretation. Throughout the ages and around the world, dyers relied on the colors obtained from plants, fungi, lichen, insects, shellfish, and rock minerals. In ancient cultures such as China and Japan, things that yielded colors were often associated with medicinal and mystical powers. A similar reverence and curiosity about colors derived from nature is growing among contemporary dyers and artists who choose to experience themselves working within the biosphere, in partnership with nature rather than trying to exploit or control it.

Those of us who dye and print with natural materials want to know how to best obtain color and use it to achieve the hues and shades we wish to see—ones that inspire our personal creative expressions. Our desire to use natural colors resonates with current environmental and ecological awareness and a need to know scientifically how to practice natural dyeing sustainably. We want to understand how dyes and mordants work and how different types of fibers react to dyes, mordants, tannins, water, heat, and ultraviolet (UV) rays. We need to become familiar with the major dye categories such as anthraquinoids, flavonoids, and the three different types of tannins and understand the colors they produce and their properties when applied with particular processes. Having very clear and precise instructions to follow helps us achieve that goal, but unless we understand the *why* behind the *how*, we won't be able to make the most intelligent decisions when changing circumstances require that recipes be altered. Organic matters (dyes and fibers) are products of the natural environment and as such are affected by soil, climate, harvesting season, and regionally specific differences, not to mention suppliers, extraction methods, conditions of storage, and transport of materials to reach the hands of dyers. Taking such factors into account, this book creates a bridge between art and science, showing us the way.

Over the past decade, I have followed a path of inquiry into natural dyes and colors and found my mentor in Michel Garcia, a botanist, horticulturist, phytochemist, historian, and natural dyer. Catharine Ellis along with many other artists and dyers joined in this mode of research and experimentation with natural materials to achieve colors on cloth or paper.

I first met Catharine in 1990 at the Penland School of Crafts in North Carolina, where she attended a class I was teaching on Japanese textile history. An accomplished weaver, she had practiced that craft since the early 1970s. After spending a week experimenting with placing stitches on cloth and then gathering them to create a resist before dyeing, it was only natural that she would think about applying weaving structure to the resist technique. She was excited to realize that she could use weft floats in weaving like the stitching threads in *shibori*. Tightening the float, she created a puckered surface, which served as a shaped resist for dyeing. When the float was removed, the integrity of the cloth's weave structure was maintained. Woven *shibori* was the perfect marriage of the weaver's and the dyer's art.

Catharine continued to experiment and discover possibilities. She introduced the idea of combining weaving and shaped-resist dyeing in two editions of *Woven Shibori*, in 2005 and 2016. In the second edition, Catharine covered a broad selection of natural dyes and generously included details of her experimentation with natural dyes and colors on selected natural fibers vis-à-vis work she developed after participating in the filming of the instructional video I produced of Michel Garcia's Natural Dye Workshop.

Catharine infuses traditional textile craft with the spirit of scientific experimentation. She loves testing and approaches tedious empirical work with patience and keen observation. She conducts extensive testing for colorfastness and color saturation in different textiles with various processes. She also grows dye

plants and creates some of her own dyes. In this age when natural dyeing has become fashionable, she goes beyond simply substituting natural for synthetic dye powder and explores the significance and potential of natural colors in her various weaving projects.

I first met Joy Boutrup in the 1990s and started co-teaching with her in the United States, Europe, and Japan. Teaching with her was like seeing the world of textile design through a different pair of glasses. She demonstrated and taught ways to understand dyes and fibers on a molecular level, to learn about their chemical reactions and bring the most out of the materials and ingredients. For example, Joy's students would never look at woven woolen fabric surfaces the same way as before. She led us to examine each step of the way that fabric can be transformed, including various ways fleece can be made into yarn, and a wide range of weaving structures and fabric-finishing processes, and then to orchestrate all the variants to create surface patterning and texturing. She has a unique knack for explaining complex textile chemistry, structures, and technologies in understandable terms. Her pointers and explanations throughout this book help readers develop a foundation for understanding natural dyeing process and practice. She has provided the backbone of Catharine's search for answers when *why* and *how* came up in her dyeing practice.

Drawing on her training in textile engineering with specialization in chemistry, Joy created a stir in Scandinavia by reintroducing industrial formulas from the early years of the Industrial Revolution. Many of her discoveries and reinventions were welcomed enthusiastically, spread to other countries, and gradually incorporated into the curriculum of textile art education. During the early 1990s she and Jason Pollen, a driving force in the Surface Design Association (SDA), co-taught workshops attended by many leading fiber artists and teachers, including Catharine. Soon there was a surge of interest in North America in adopting industrial processes and understanding the chemical ingredients of the dyeing process.

Joy brings to this book her vast knowledge and her enthusiasm for research into the history of textile technique. She and Catharine offer an essential selection of tested and proven recipes for mordanting, dyeing, and printing that are applicable to all dyers, from beginner to experienced. They present concise, detailed, and objective explanations of *why* specific recipes are selected and used. Readers then can choose *how* to dye with specific materials available to them for a particular purpose. All the recipes utilize environmentally benign and readily available chemicals and substances and are based on the best of historical and contemporary practices. With Catharine, the fiber artist, and Joy, the textile scientist, as your companions and guides, you will enjoy encountering and beginning to unlock the mysteries of natural dyeing.

—YOSHIKO IWAMOTO WADA

Introduction

Joy Boutrup and I met in 1997 at Penland School of Crafts in North Carolina. Joy was teaching classes on the technical aspects of printing and textile finishing. I was a student. That first introduction has led to a valued friendship and years of collaboration, influencing my own studio work and eventually leading to our collaborative teaching. Joy's knowledge of textile science, history, and theory are complemented by my own studio practice, which includes investigation both of weaving and dyeing. For several years, we have been using and teaching exclusively about, and with, natural dyes.

While working on her textile-engineering degree in 1970, Joy researched natural dyes in Germany. She analyzed historical dyed textiles and had contact with Helmut Schweppe, author of *Handbuch der Naturfarbstoffe*. Joy began dyeing then and has continued to grow and use natural dyes for the silk yarns in her reconstructions of historical braids.

My first exposure to natural dyeing came in the early 1970s, when there was little real information available. Much of the process seemed haphazard, and unsafe mordants were used without caution. I shortly abandoned natural dyes and spent many years mastering the use of synthetic dyes. Ten years ago, wanting to use safer and more-sustainable dye practices, I decided to investigate natural dyeing once again.

In 2008 I met the influential dye expert Michel Garcia. It was a critical time, as I was just beginning to explore the possibility of changing my dye practice. He showed me natural dye colors and processes that I didn't know were possible. I was inspired and began a long series of experiments in my own studio. With Joy's help, I was able to decipher some of the conflicting information I encountered and to appreciate the underlying principles of natural dyeing. Her knowledge of fibers, dye chemistry, and experience with printing techniques was invaluable.

Some of the references that Joy identified included handbooks written by and for the industrial dye trade in the early twentieth century. Natural dyes were still being used in industry at that time, and there was knowledge of the chemistry applied in the processes. *The Principles and Practice of Textile Printing*, first published in 1912, was written by two men: Edmund Knecht and James Best Fothergill; one was a scientist and the other was a practitioner. They understood theory, tested recipes, and observed results. Much of their writing is more technical than I could have deciphered without Joy's help.

Joy and I have written the book that I would have found most useful 10 years ago. Simply having a "recipe" was never enough. I wanted to understand "why" certain processes work and the principles on which they were based. Once I understood those principles, I was free to adjust and experiment. That is the beginning of mastering a craft.

In addition to the basics of mordanting and dyeing, we have included useful older techniques, such as printing with indigo, discharge of indigo dye, and direct printing of mordant dyes. We have given a "facelift" to these old processes, making them suitable for today's dyer. After testing and observation, we have recommended recipes and processes that we consider the best options.

The book is organized with technical information and the "principles" of natural dyeing presented up front. Each chapter addresses a different topic, including fibers, mordants, dyes, dyeing, printing, indigo, and finishing. Samples produced as a result of actual dye tests are used to illustrate the book throughout.

All recipes are collected together in chapter 11. Each of the recipes that we have chosen has been tested many times for dye projects both large and small. The book is a practical approach for the contemporary dyer. A separate vocabulary section further explains some technical terms that might not be part of a dyer's vocabulary.

This book is intended as a handbook that should live in the studio for easy and frequent reference. The dyer is encouraged to use the recipes, carefully observe results, and adjust as needed. Outcomes will differ depending on the textile, the water source, the dye source, and the dyer.

The more experience I have as a dyer, the more I realize that there is no single "absolute" way to dye. Natural dyeing is a "practice" that is supported by best available knowledge and experience, but it is still an empirical science and much has not been studied conclusively. Research in the field of dye chemistry continues around the world on many different levels.

We have explained processes to the best of our knowledge and understanding, based on available science, historical documents, and experience. Natural dyeing continues to surprise me, but its palette is always pleasing and harmonious. Every project has the potential to provide new information and leave the dyer with a deeper understanding.

It is our hope that dyers use this book as a resource. We challenge all dyers to continue learning from practice, research, and each other in the pursuit of safe and sustainable dyeing.

—CATHARINE ELLIS

Acknowledgments

We would sincerely like to thank:

Our readers, who critically examined the text and recipes, asked questions, made comments, and, in general, challenged us: Amanda Thatch, Ana Lisa Hedstrom, Bhakti Ziek, Diane deSouza, Donna Brown, Elin Noble, Sheri McNerthy, and Wendy Weiss.

The teachers of natural dyeing and their students, who tested early versions of recipes in their classes: Amy Putansu (Haywood Community College), Kim Eichler-Messmer (Kansas City Art Institute), and Rowland Ricketts (Indiana University).

Dominique Cardon. In additional to writing the most important resource book on natural dye sources, Dominique offered encouragement and important advice.

Yoshiko Wada and Charllotte Kwon. Their commitment to natural dyes has been an inspiration and a driving force in the field.

Bethanne Knudson and the Oriole Mill for sharing their incredibly beautiful fabrics for dye testing.

Kent Stewart, who patiently read through many, many versions of this text.

Natural dyers everywhere, the greatest inspiration of all.

CHAPTER 1
Dyeing Textiles

Natural dyeing is a process of coloring textiles with dyes from plants or insects. Until the middle of the nineteenth century, all textiles were dyed with natural colorants, since there was no other source of color. The first synthetic dyes were developed in 1856, but the use of natural dyes continued in industry for another 50 years. Dye guilds had strict standards of color and dye quality. Any deviation would likely result in diminished business or even expulsion from professional dyers' organizations. Professional dyers studied and refined processes of mordanting and dye application. Home dyers, who were not subject to the same stringent rules, often used locally available dye plants, settling for what was available even if that meant a limited color palette and lesser-quality dye.

Color was valuable in a way that is hard for us to understand today. Some colors were simply not within reach to certain economic communities or in certain geographic areas. In Japan, rare colors such as brilliant pink from safflower or deep purple from gromwell root were highly valued. Despite the fact that some of their dyes were very fugitive, these plants were the only means of achieving such a hue.

In the past, dyers often utilized toxic or environmentally harmful chemicals such as lead acetate, chromium, and arsenic in order to achieve desired color effects, especially in textile printing. Today's natural dyers must seek to attain the best results possible in an environmentally sustainable and responsible way.

Textiles

Natural textile fibers consist either of protein or cellulose. Both are long chains of connected units. Protein units are made of amino acids, while cellulose units are chains of beta-glucose. All fibers, whether protein or cellulose, consist of crystalline structures of dense, highly organized chains and amorphous structures of looser, less orderly organized chains. The highly structured, crystalline parts do not allow easy penetration of water or dyes into the fiber. However, the amorphous parts allow easy entry, and this is where mordants and dyes can penetrate.

Each natural fiber is made of varying amounts of crystalline and amorphous structures, and the ratio of crystalline to amorphous structures is a factor in determining how easily the fiber will dye. Wool is primarily amorphous inside while the scales are highly crystalline. Silk, cotton, and linen are more crystalline throughout.

Dyeing Textiles

Dyes, and Pigments

In the textile field there is a clear distinction between dyes and pigments. Dyes are soluble in the medium used for dyeing. A dye is able to penetrate into the fiber, and it has little effect on the surface properties of the textile. Dyes are transparent and will mix with the base colors of the fiber. It is not possible to hide or cover spots or imperfections in the textile with dye.

Pigments, on the other hand, are not soluble in water. They are adhered to the surface with the help of a binder. The presence of pigments on the surface will change the gloss or sheen of the textile. Pigments are not transparent and can, in sufficient concentrations, hide underlying colors. The binder can also change the hand, or feel, of the textile.

Natural dyes come from a variety of sources, including various parts of plants, insects, mollusks, lichens, and mushrooms. There are many conditions that affect the final dyed color. For instance, the color produced by a dye source varies considerably depending on its growing conditions, harvesting, drying, and storage. Since each dye source contains several dyes with slightly different hues, the varying conditions and treatments of the dye can potentially change each one of them. Similarly, the variables during dyeing, such as temperature or acidity, also influence the final hue.

Most natural dyes are readily soluble in water. The two exceptions are indigo and classical purple, which are "vat" dyes. In their extracted form, they are pigments and insoluble in water. Through alkaline reduction, the dye changes into a soluble compound that is able to penetrate the fiber. Through oxidation, which is the opposite of reduction, the original dye forms again inside the fiber after dyeing and is permanently attached.

Most of the soluble dyes are considered mordant dyes. During dyeing, the water-soluble dye moves into the fiber, where it combines with a mordant, which is a metal salt such as aluminum or iron. The combination of dye and mordant forms an insoluble compound, called a lake. The dye lake is relatively permanent and resistant to washing. The lake can be formed only in neutral or slightly alkaline conditions and cannot form in an acidic environment.

Dyes that attach to wool fiber without a mordant (e.g., black walnut and certain tannin dyes) do not form insoluble lakes. Instead, their attachment is one of chemical affinity, and they are often dyed in acidic conditions.

The overall goal of dyeing is to encourage as much dye as possible to evenly penetrate the fibers, where it then becomes fixed. When dyeing is complete there should be a minimal amount of dye left on the surface of the fiber or in the water.

The dye lakes, the insoluble compounds formed by mordants and mordant dyes, can also be formed outside the fibers. In this case they become insoluble pigments. These pigments can be fastened to a variety of surfaces with appropriate binders.

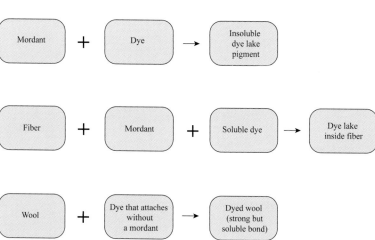

CHAPTER 2
Fibers

Successful natural dyeing requires an understanding of the fibers themselves and the challenges involved in applying both mordants and dyes. This chapter includes an overview of the natural fibers in relation to dyeing, and recommendations for preparing the textiles for dyeing. Specific recipes for scouring and cleaning textiles are in chapter 11.

Natural dyes are most effective on natural materials. Protein and cellulose are the two major categories of natural and regenerated fibers. Both can be dyed, but the approach to fiber preparation and mordanting is different for each.

Fibers that come from animals consist of protein structures and are referred to as protein fibers. These include silk, wool, hair, fur, feathers, and soy fiber. The most common are from domesticated sheep and silkworms. Protein fibers have the greatest affinity for natural dyes and are the easiest to dye. They form strong bonds with mordants, which in turn bind with the dyes.

Cellulose fibers are derived from plants: stems, barks, or seed bolls. The most common are cotton and linen, but this category also includes hemp, pineapple, sisal, ramie, and regenerated fibers such as rayon, Tencel®, and Lyocell®. Cellulose fibers do not have an affinity for mordants nor do they form the same type of bonds with the mordants that protein does. For this reason, tannin is used in the mordanting of cellulose for immersion dyeing. (The cellulose printing process uses mordants in a concentrated form that precipitate onto the fiber without the use of tannin.) With proper mordanting, cellulose fibers can be dyed successfully.

WHY IS PROTEIN EASIER TO DYE THAN CELLULOSE?

Protein fibers are easy to dye by using both synthetic and natural dyes. Proteins readily absorb and react with both acids and alkalis. Within the molecular structure of protein fibers are amino groups (alkaline), carboxyl groups (acid), and OH groups. The presence of both amino and carboxyl groups ensures that the fiber will react with both acids and alkalis. The amino groups readily react with acids, while the carboxyl groups will react with alkalis. In general, the OH groups are relatively inactive and don't react with acids and alkalis.

When wool and silk are immersed in water with a pH lower than 5, the fiber becomes positively charged and attracts negatively charged acid dyes, such as cochineal, and tannin-based dyes. Once they are attracted and bound, they are relatively washfast but sensitive to very alkaline conditions.

The mordants are metal ions that are always positively charged. They bind to the uncharged amino groups in the protein. The resulting bond between the fiber and the mordant is relatively strong. The presence of acid, such as cream of tartar, during the mordanting process will slow the absorption of the mordants and assist to level the distribution of the mordant in the textile.

While the important bond to protein fibers is the one to the amino groups, cellulose is primarily made up of OH groups that cannot bind to most dyes or mordants, requiring a different approach to mordanting and dyeing.

Wool

Wool fibers are made of a unique, open-structured (amorphous) core called the cortex that is covered with a layer of overlapping, compact scales. Because the scales on the surface of wool are water repellent, it is often necessary to add a wetting agent in order to wet the fibers thoroughly. The scales open when the wool fiber swells in water. When the wool is heated in water the core (cortex) swells, causing the scales to open up more, making room for mordants and dyes to penetrate between the scales and into the fiber cortex, where there is plenty of space for the mordants and dyes.

Wool is usually mordanted and dyed in a heated immersion bath and is seldom used in printing processes because of the challenge of getting the dye and mordant past the scales and into the fiber.

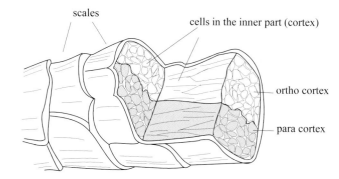

Drawing of a wool fiber. The inner cortex has two parts: the orthocortex and paracortex, each of which has different densities. Coarse wool and hair fibers are likely to have a medulla, a hollow space in the center of the cortex, which cannot absorb dye. Fine wool has no medulla.

Wool in natural white and gray tones, mordanted with alum and dyed with cochineal and weld.

Various breeds of wool react differently when dyed. The thickness, overlap, and size of the scales vary from one breed of sheep to another. Some hair fibers, such as camel, angora and alpaca, have air-filled cells called the medulla, which do not dye at all and can cause a whitish look to the color. Superwash wools have been treated to prevent the wool from felting. The scales of superwash wool are partially removed or are covered with a thin layer of polymer. The polymer covers the scales to prevent felting but also dyes more readily than the wool. Sometimes both of these treatments are used. Either treatment will result in wool that absorbs dye easily, but the results are sometimes uneven.

Some wool fibers, in the initial cleaning, have been treated with a strong acid and heated in order to remove/carbonize plant material entangled in the fibers. Usually the acid is neutralized before the wool comes to the market, but the neutralization is not always complete. If carbonized wool is not properly neutralized, the textile will be too acidic for the formation of the dye-mordant lake in the fibers, and the textile will not dye.

When wool is wet, it is mechanically weak and subject to stretching and felting unless handled with great care. While in a mildly acidic solution (pH 5), the wool will be the strongest and less apt to be damaged by rubbing or agitation. For this reason, mildly acidic detergents are used in the cleaning process. Mordant baths are also mildly acidic, which helps protect the wool. When dyeing, the temperature is kept below a boil. Boiling is always damaging to wool since it dissolves some of the proteins and molecular bonds. We recommend that any color mixing be done in a single dye bath (except for combinations with indigo) rather than overdyeing, which would subject the wool to multiple dye baths and create additional opportunities for damage. Slow, unheated mordant and dye baths are options that will be discussed.

Wool is naturally colored in shades of brown, tan, gray, and near black. Although white wool has become the industry standard, the use of naturally colored wools can expand the palette of dye and the depth of color when using natural dyes.

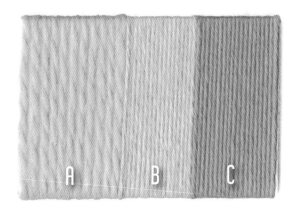

A. wool, B. alpaca, C. superwash wool. All fibers are mordanted with alum and dyed with cochineal and weld. The absence of scales on superwash wool allows greater absorption of dye.

Fibers

Silk

Silk fibers, in their raw state directly from the cocoon, are double-stranded, parallel protein fibers. The fibers are made of very crystalline fibroin surrounded by sericin (silk gum). Sericin is an amorphous, gluelike protein substance that holds the two fibers together. Silk is generally degummed, a process where the sericin is removed, resulting in a silk that is smooth, soft, and lustrous. Raw silk, which has not been degummed, is stiff with a matte surface. It will absorb more dye than degummed silk because of the amorphous layer

of sericin. Silk organza is made from silk that has not been degummed. It contains sericin, which makes it stiff and prevents the open weave from sliding. Organza will, due to the content of sericin, dye a deeper color than silk *habotai*, for example, which has been totally degummed and does not contain sericin.

Sometimes silk yarns that are sold as degummed have not been thoroughly scoured and may still contain some sericin. If dyed in this state, very irregular or spotty dyeing will result since the mordant and dye will

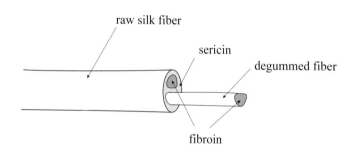

Drawing of a silk fiber. The amorphous sericin absorbs more dye than the degummed, smooth, crystalline fibroin fibers.

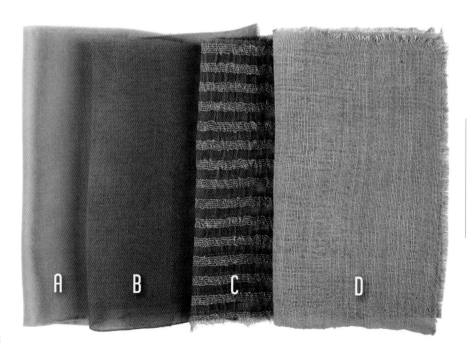

Silk fabrics, mordanted with alum and dyed with cutch: A. scoured silk broadcloth, B. silk organza (with sericin), C. scoured and unscoured, silk, combined in the weave, D. wild Indian silk.

bind unevenly due to the uneven presence of sericin. If a silk yarn reacts this way, we recommend that it be thoroughly degummed prior to mordanting and dyeing in order to achieve uniform dyeing.

Tussah and other wild silks are more crystalline and absorb less dye and mordant than other silks. They cannot be totally degummed. Consequently, they will always contain some sericin, which makes them susceptible to color changes or spotting when exposed to water drops or steam ironing.

Silk is a protein and is usually treated as such in the mordant and dye processes. Because silk fibers are much thinner than wool and because they do not have scales on the surface, silk does not require heat in the mordanting process, and it is dyed at lower temperatures. Silk is more tolerant of alkalinity and less tolerant of acids than wool, and it can also be mordanted like cellulose.

Cotton

Cotton is almost pure cellulose. It is made of relatively short staple lengths that are formed as twisted ribbons with a kidney-shaped cross section. On the cuticle (or skin) of the fiber is a waxy layer that is typically removed during wet processing. The wax is usually found only in raw cotton and in some unmercerized yarns. If not removed by scouring, the wax will prevent the penetration of mordant and dye.

The quality of cotton fiber directly affects how well it will dye. Mature, high-quality cotton has thick walls of cellulose, which will readily accept mordants and dye. Immature, poor-quality, or "dead" cotton has thin walls that are not as receptive to mordants or dye. The lumen is the hollow canal that runs inside the length of the fiber. When the cotton plant is growing, the lumen is full of sap. Once the cotton begins to dry and is harvested, the sap evaporates and the cell collapses, forming the kidney-shaped cross section of the fiber.

In 1844 John Mercer, an English dyer and textile chemist, discovered that when cotton was treated with lye (sodium hydroxide solution) the color yield from natural dyes increased. The use of lye caused the fiber to swell and changed the cellulose fiber to sodium cellulose, which has a more open structure and a higher affinity for dyes. Nearly 50 years later, the process was improved by treating woven fabric under tension. In addition to accepting dyes more readily, the tension prevented the fibers from shrinking and caused the cotton to straighten, become stronger, round in cross section, and more lustrous. This process was named mercerization in honor of John Mercer.

Cotton yarns can be mercerized, but cotton is typically mercerized after weaving, in the cloth state. The mercerization treatment is used only on clean, mature fibers that are free of waxes or sizing. The dyer can be confident that mercerized cotton is of a high quality and will readily accept mordants and dyes.

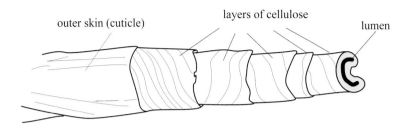

outer skin (cuticle)   layers of cellulose   lumen

Drawing of a cotton fiber. A narrow lumen, surrounded by many layers of cellulose, is found in high-quality cotton fibers.

Linen and Hemp

Linen and hemp are compound bast fibers; that is, a bundle of fibers. The compound is made of relatively short fibers, called "elementary," with compact crystalline structures. These fibers are attached to each other with calcium-containing pectins. Dye penetrates the amorphous pectin first and very often will not enter the elementary fiber, resulting in "ring dyeing." Dyeing bast fibers requires patience and increased dyeing time when compared to other fibers to ensure that the mordant and dye penetrate the very crystalline fibers. Indigo dyeing can be especially challenging since a vat dye is more apt to remain on the surface.

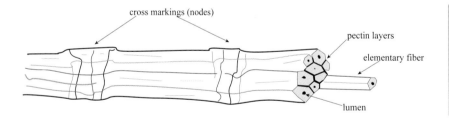

cross markings (nodes)

pectin layers

elementary fiber

lumen

Drawing of a linen fiber. The elementary fibers are very smooth and held together by layers of pectin. The surface of the compound fiber is also smooth and shiny. The nodes are characteristic of bast (stem) fibers. Hemp has a very similar structure and appearance.

Rough mechanical treatment will damage bast fibers. They have a low tolerance for bending or flexing and should not be machine washed. Traditionally, linen was cleaned by boiling or pounding flat.

In the initial processing of the fiber, retting breaks down some of the pectins, but the remaining ones contain calcium and are important to the strength of the fiber. Linen and hemp should be cleaned and wetted out (see chapter 2, page 23) only with a neutral detergent. Strong alkaline detergents will damage pectins, separating the bast into elementary fibers, which leaves the textiles weaker and less smooth and shiny.

The natural color of linen and hemp is gray or yellow as a result of the retting process. A white linen or hemp textile indicates that it has been bleached.

A. Natural linen, B. bleached linen, mordanted with aluminum and dyed by using weld and madder.

Ramie

Ramie is a compound bast fiber and is the strongest of the cellulose fibers. In its raw state, ramie is stiff with pectins. The pectin is normally removed by alkaline boiling before spinning. This leaves the long elementary fibers shiny and soft. The elementary fibers of ramie are three to five times longer than those of linen and hemp. They can be spun as individual fibers. Because there is no pectin holding the fibers together, ramie is not as sensitive to washing or to the use of alkaline detergents. Ramie is pure white and readily accepts dye.

Regenerated Cellulose Fibers

VISCOSE RAYON

Viscose rayon is a regenerated cellulose fiber produced by the viscose method. The raw material, the cellulose that's being "regenerated," is wood pulp. Cellulose is dissolved and extruded, and the extruded fibers are coagulated. The viscose process is not environmentally friendly, since the chemicals used are not recyclable and create a great deal of waste. The quality of viscose can vary considerably depending on the producer. There are only a few brand names with a guarantee of high quality. In general, viscose fibers are relatively

amorphous, weak, and apt to shrink and crinkle. They are very sensitive to strong alkali and might not tolerate the alkalinity of indigo vats or indigo printing.

Modal® is a brand name for a high-quality regenerated cellulose fiber produced by a modified viscose method. It has a higher crystallinity, strength, and resistance to alkali than normal viscose.

TENCEL® AND LYOCELL®

Tencel and Lyocell are regenerated cellulose fibers produced by the lyocell production method, where the chemicals and water used in the fiber production are recycled almost 100 percent. The source of cellulose is primarily wood pulp. It is considered to be more environmentally friendly than viscose rayon as a result of the manufacturing process. These fibers are highly crystalline, stronger than cotton even when wet, and dye readily.

"BAMBOO FIBERS"

So-called bamboo fibers are regenerated cellulose fibers produced from bamboo cellulose. Most of these products on the market are produced by using the viscose method. Only a few brands are using the cleaner lyocell production method. The cellulose in bamboo is linked to antiseptic compounds, and it is theorized, but not proven, that it retains its antiseptic properties in the fiber.

Cellulose yarns: A. Tencel, B. unmercerized cotton, C. mercerized cotton, D. natural brown cotton, E. bleached linen, F. natural linen. All fibers were treated with tannin, mordanted with aluminum, and dyed with madder.

Preparing Textiles for Dyeing and Printing

SOAPS AND DETERGENTS

Each type of fiber has an "ideal" pH where it is strongest and "happiest." The ideal pH for protein fibers is about pH 5.0. Cellulose fibers are tolerant of mild acid or alkaline conditions and are usually left at a neutral pH of 7.0. Understanding these preferences will make it easier for the dyer to choose the correct approach to cleaning and scouring.

Soap is alkaline, and the pH can vary from 8.0 to 12.0. Soap is made from natural ingredients by combining fats or oils with sodium or potassium salts such as lye (sodium hydroxide) or soda ash (sodium carbonate). These include olive oil soaps, Castile soaps, or milk soaps. Soaps should not be used for scouring. If they react with calcium or magnesium in hard water, they will form fatty substances that coat the fiber and subsequently will resist mordants and dyes.

Detergents are made from synthetic ingredients, and the pH can vary widely, from slightly acidic to very alkaline. Laundry detergents generally are mixtures of many ingredients and are often highly alkaline. Detergents that are pH neutral or slightly acidic are recommended for scouring and cleaning all textiles. Appropriate commercially available products include Orvus Paste™, Synthrapol™, and neutral dishwashing liquids. If not rinsed out completely, the neutral detergents will have no detrimental effect on subsequent processes.

Natural detergents include yucca root or soapwort (*Saponaria*). Both these natural detergents contain saponins, which are poisonous to fish and insects when released in sewage or stream waters. They are not more environmentally friendly than synthetic detergents.

SCOURING/CLEANING/WETTING

Before fibers are dyed, any contaminants such as dirt, grease, or sizing must be removed so that the mordant and dye are able to freely penetrate the textile. True scouring usually includes heat or boiling. The scouring process is specific to the fiber and the contaminants present in the textile. Without scouring, dyeing will inevitably be uneven because the mordant and some of the dye will remain on the surface rather than penetrate into the fiber.

Cleaning is simply a thorough washing and includes a neutral detergent.

In addition to being clean, all textiles must be thoroughly moistened, called "wetting out," in order to ensure even penetration of the mordant and dye into the fibers. A small amount of neutral detergent may be used as a wetting agent in order to decrease surface tension of the liquid, allowing water to more readily penetrate the textile.

Linen fabric: Sample A was not completely wetted out prior to dyeing with indigo, although it "appeared" to be wet. Sample B is thoroughly cleaned and wetted out before dyeing.

Fibers

Wool

Raw, unwashed wool fleece or other animal fibers must be thoroughly scoured to remove dirt and grease before mordanting or dying. These fibers can contain 30 percent or more of their weight in dirt, wax, sweat, and mineral salts. Consult with reliable sources for the best process to clean raw fleece.

Wool that has been previously scoured to remove grease and dirt may still contain spinning oils, which are often added during the industrial spinning process, and must be washed in a neutral detergent. If no oils are present, the textile needs only to be wetted before mordanting and dyeing. Alpaca and other hair fibers can be treated the same as wool.

Silk

Silk is scoured in a heated alkaline solution only to remove sericin. Otherwise, wetting out is the only preparation necessary prior to dyeing.

Cotton

Unmercerized cotton, along with other cellulose yarns and textiles, may contain wax, spinning oils, starch, or other sizing. Scouring in detergent and soda ash removes most of these substances. Scouring does not remove starch. If starch is present, this is usually a result of warp sizing that leaves the textile stiff. Soak the textile in a wheat bran solution overnight. The enzymes in the bran will break down the starch, which is then removed in the rinsing.

Mercerized cottons typically do not have sizing or starches, but they may have spinning oils, which must be removed by scouring.

Fabrics that are prepared for dyeing (PFD) or ready to dye (RTD) usually have no starches, sizes, oils, or finishes, but they will benefit from cleaning in a neutral detergent.

Refer to recipes 1, 2, 3, and 4.

CHAPTER 3
Dyes

A dye is a soluble colorant, or a colorant that can be made soluble, that is used to color textiles. This chapter describes some of the most important natural dyes and how they are categorized. It includes extraction methods used for dye source materials and specific information about the individual dyes so that the dyer can optimize each dye. We also discuss tannins and offer suggestions for gathering local dye plants. General dye instructions are found in chapter 5.

Sources of Dyes

- Plants: leaves, flowers, roots, bark, wood, fruit
- Lichens and mushrooms (usually for protein fibers only)
- Scale insects (reds only)
- Mollusks (purple only)

Almost any plant will produce some color, but the requirements for a good dye plant are that the color be strong and reasonably permanent. The dye must also be resistant to washing and light. Any dyed textile will lose some of its intensity over time, but the best dyes will maintain their integrity for the life of the textile. For the most part, edible plants do not contain dyes suitable for textiles, though some are suitable as food dyes. Indiscriminate use of fugitive dyes, which will quickly fade when exposed to light or washing, has the potential for damaging the reputation not only of the one dyer, but of all dyers. Care should be taken in choosing dyes and methods of applications for contemporary textile work.

Accurate lightfast testing of dyes can be conducted by using the guidelines in chapter 10.

Dyes

Names and Categories of Plants and Dyes

Most natural dyes come from plants, though there are a few that come from insects (cochineal, lac, kermes) and only one traditional dye that comes from an animal (mollusk purple). The purple dyes are rare and generally unavailable to dyers and thus will not be addressed as a source of dye. The dyes this book focuses on are from available plants and red-producing insects that will result in long-lasting color.

Each dye source (plant or insect) has one or more common names and a scientific Latin name that includes the genus and species. There may be several plants in the same genus that contain similar dyes, and familiarity with the scientific name will assist you in correctly categorizing and identifying the dyes. When *tinctoria* is a plant's species name, it indicates that the plant is traditionally used for dyeing, such as *Isatis tinctoria* (woad). The species name *officinale* indicates a medicinal plant, such as *Rheum officinale* (Chinese rhubarb). Many medicinal plants are also good for dyeing.

The plant or the insect itself is not the dye. The dyes are contained within the plants or insects from which they are sourced. All dye sources contain multiple dye compounds, and each of the compounds within the plant has its own chemical name, such as luteolin, alizarin, or juglone. Familiarity with the different dye compounds in each source makes it easier to understand similarities and differences among the dye sources. Also, remember that the handling and processing of the raw material during harvest, storage, and extraction and in the dye process may shift the balance between these different dyes and result in slightly different hues.

All dyes are classified in two primary categories:

- Chemical group, which defines the main chemical compound in the dye.
- Dye class, which indicates how the dye is applied to the textile.

Major Chemical Groups

The dyes in each chemical group share very specific properties. These are the major chemical groups of dyes and some examples of dyes within each group.

- Anthraquinoids: most of the red dyes, including the insect dyes and most of the root dyes.

- Naphthoquinoids: henna and walnut.

- Flavonoids: most of the yellow dyes.

- Indigoids: indigo (from which the group receives its name) and mollusk purple.

- Gallotannins: These are mostly colorless or yellow.

- Condensed tannins: These are usually brown or reddish brown.

Many dye plants contain dyes from more than one of these chemical groups. For instance, pomegranate rind contains both gallotannin and a flavonoid dye. Madder root contains both anthraquinoid dyes and tannins.

ANTHRAQUINOIDS

The word "anthraquinoid" is a combination of two words referring to chemical structures. The first part comes from *anthracen*, a carbon structure consisting of three connected rings. The second part is from *quinon*, which is oxygen bound to carbon on the middle ring. Most of the natural red dyes have this structure in the dye molecule and are called anthraquinoids. Anthraquinoid dyes are some of the most colorfast dyes of both the natural and synthetic dyes. Anthraquinoids can be used as mordant dyes, are sometimes applied directly, and are suitable for one-bath acid dyeing.

NAPHTHOQUINOIDS

The word is derived from *naphthen*, a chemical structure consisting of two connected carbon rings, and *quinon*, which is oxygen attached to one of the rings. Dyes containing this structure within the dyestuff molecule are referred to as naphthoquinoid dyes. These dyes can be used as mordant dyes, are sometimes used for direct application, and are suitable for one-bath acid dyeing.

FLAVONOIDS

This group's name comes from the Latin word *flavus*, which means yellow. Flavonoids are the source of many of the bright colors in plants and are the most important source of yellow dyes. There are several thousand flavonoids, but only a few of them are recognized as good dyes. These include luteolin, quercetin, apigenin, and several others. Flavonoids always require the use of a mordant.

INDIGOIDS

These are a group of vat dyes that have a chemical structure similar to indigo. Once extracted from the plant (indigo), or from the shellfish (murex), the dye is insoluble in water and is applied with the use of a reduction vat.

TANNINS

- **Gallotannins** are a group of tannins that are compounds of tannic acid and ellagic acid combined with sugars. They are primarily colorless or yellow. Examples include gallnut, sumac, myrobalan, and pomegranate.

- **Condensed tannins** are a group of tannins that are compounds of cathechin or flavan. The condensed tannins are primarily brown or reddish brown and are used as a source of dye. Examples include cutch, quebracho, and chestnut.

Chapter 3
Dyes

Major Classes of Dyes

"Dye class" refers to how the dyes are applied to the textile.

DYES APPLIED DIRECTLY WITHOUT A MORDANT

There is a group of dyes that will fix onto protein fibers without the aid of mordants. There is not a specific name for this group of dyes. Some of these are acid dyes, some are basic dyes, and some are oxidation dyes. They attach to protein fibers by means of affinity and an electrical attraction between the dye and the fiber. This group of natural dyes includes henna, cochineal, black walnut husks, and some tannins. There are a very limited number of dyes that work in this way. They are most effective on wool and usually less effective on silk. Cellulose fibers do not have the same potential electrical charge, and these dyes are generally not suitable for dyeing cellulose.

The terms "direct dye" and "substantive dye" are often used to describe these natural dyes, but since these terms are primarily used to describe classes of synthetic dyes, we have chosen to use the category of "dyes applied directly without a mordant" to eliminate confusion.

There are other dyes that can be applied to protein fiber without the use of a mordant, provided tannin and acid are present. These are applied as one-bath acid dyes and are described in chapter 5.

MORDANT DYES

Mordant dyes, the largest class, include most natural dyes. They require the use of a mordant in order to be fixed into the fibers and to be resistant to light, water, and washing. These dyes include most of the yellow and red dyes.

VAT DYES

Vat dyes are not soluble in water and must be applied to the fiber by means of a process of reduction and oxidation. Indigo and mollusk purple dyes belong to this class of dyes. Since vat dyes behave differently from other classes of dyes, chapter 6 will address the use of indigo.

Sample fabrics, constructed of wool and cotton, dyed with henna and cochineal. No mordant was used. Dyes that are applied by using immersion baths without a mordant will attach strongly to wool and weakly to silk and will only lightly stain cellulose.

Sources of Dye

Dyes can be sourced in several different forms:

- Fresh plants.

- Dried plants or dried insects. Most dye material can be dried successfully and stored for future use. Dried plants are more concentrated per weight of material than fresh plants. Once dry and carefully stored, dye materials have a nearly unlimited shelf life.

- Extracts: Dye extracts are a concentrated, water-soluble form of natural dye and are produced in a controlled laboratory setting. They require no further extraction. The extraction methods originally used to make the extracts vary, as do their strength and purity. They may be in either liquid or a dry powder form.

Extraction of Dye from Dye Source Materials

- Optimizing the extraction of dye from the source materials will result in the best quality and quantity of dye.

Break, grind, or pulverize the source material into the smallest pieces possible. More dye will be extracted from finer particles.

Soak the material in water in order to soften the plant material and prepare it for extraction. This is most important for wood, roots, stems, and bark, which benefit from overnight extractions. It is not necessary to presoak flowers, leaves, or other soft or finely ground materials. When some woods are soaked in alcohol, different dyes are extracted from the plant material, potentially producing different dye colors.

The extraction/decoction of the dye is done in a heated water bath. Some dyes may be boiled but others (such as madder, *Rubia tinctorium*) are sensitive to color change at high temperatures. After soaking the material for the appropriate amount of time, heat the bath slowly to the suggested temperature. Maintain the bath at that temperature until the extraction is complete and the plant material sinks to the bottom of the pot. This may take only 30 minutes for fresh leaves or flowers, but an hour or more for dense bark and roots. During the extraction, an enzymatic process separates the plant sugars and dissolves the dyes.

When the extraction has been completed, strain and filter the source material from the bath. Some source material may be extracted a second time to ensure that all the dye has been released. The source material can be placed in a net bag for easy removal from the bath. Some dyes, especially those that dye directly, benefit from allowing the source materials to remain in the bath while the textile is being dyed.

Extraction recommendations that are specific to a plant or insect can be found in this chapter, listed under the individual dye. These include temperatures, pH adjustments, or both. General dyeing instructions for all fibers can be found in chapter 5.

Dyes

Specific Dyes

Madder (*Rubia tinctorium*): whole roots, chopped roots, finely ground roots, and extract.

All the dyes chosen for inclusion and discussion in this book are highly recommended for their lightfastness and washfastness. They are considered the classical dyes and have been used commercially through history, and they continue to be available today. Though not an exhaustive list, it is a representative selection of chemical groups, dye classes, and colors. Each of the dyes exhibits a great deal of versatility. Some of the dyes are more suitable for use on protein, especially those that are applied without a mordant.

Having a limited number of dyes does not necessarily restrict the palette. Dye colors can be mixed in the dye pot, or textiles can be overdyed to create new colors. Some dyes may be available locally while others will need to be sourced from suppliers. All dyes should be subjected to wash and lightfast testing in order to verify their durability.

The range of suggested dye quantities, expressed as a percentage based on the fiber weight, is dependent on the desired depth of color and the quality of the dye. All dye quantities are based on the weight of dry textile prior to dyeing. This is described as "weight of fiber" or "w.o.f." Dyes from different sources or different harvests can vary dramatically in strength and hue.

DRY ROOTS

EXTRACTS

A comparison of madder dye from different suppliers/ sources on aluminum mordanted ramie. Top row: dried roots @ 50% w.o.f., bottom row: madder extract @ 10% w.o.f.

RED DYES

The red dyes are anthraquinoid dyes. They are sourced from insects or roots, produce strong color, and are lightfast and washfast. There are a limited number of these red dyes, making them some of the most valuable of the natural dyes.

Cochineal (*Dactylopius coccus*)

Source:	Cochineal is the scale insect that lives on the prickly pear cactus. The insect is native to Central and South America, and dried insects are exported worldwide.
Chemical group:	Anthraquinoid
Primary dyestuff:	Carminic acid
Class of dye:	Cochineal is used without a mordant as an acid dye on wool and as a mordant dye for both protein and cellulose.
Colors obtained:	Fuchsia pinks, purples, and reds
Amount of dye:	1–2% cochineal extract or 5–20% ground cochineal insects

Extraction: Measure and grind whole cochineal insects to a very fine consistency with a mortar and pestle or a designated coffee grinder. Cover the ground insects with water, bring to a boil, and simmer for approximately 60 minutes. Strain the liquid through a fine-mesh screen; the strained liquid will be used in the dye bath. The ground cochineal that is collected in the filter may be boiled a second time in order to release additional dye.

Dyeing: Add water to the strained dye liquid to achieve the volume required to dye the textile. Add the textile and increase the heat to a temperature suitable for that textile. Continue dyeing for an hour or until the desired color is reached. Cochineal is very pH sensitive and will react to changes in pH. The presence of acid will shift the color toward the red, while an alkaline will move the color toward the purple. Traditional dyers added the juice of a lemon in the dye bath to shift the color on protein textiles. Citric acid (approximately 5% w.o.f. to achieve ≈pH 3.5–4.0) or cream of tartar (approximately 6% w.o.f. to achieve ≈pH 5.0) is recommended. Vinegar is usually not acidic enough to shift the color. A true scarlet can be achieved by using a tin pre-mordant or by adding a small amount of tin (3%) and cream of tartar (6%) to the dye bath.

The color can be shifted toward purple with ammonia or soda ash as a post-dye alkaline pH adjuster, but a more stable purple color will result by using a very small amount of iron (less than 1%) as a post-dye treatment.

DO NOT USE CREAM OF TARTAR OR CITRIC ACID WHEN DYEING MORDANTED CELLULOSE.

The strong acids will remove the mordant from the cellulose textile and result in a much-lighter color. Since color shifts so easily with pH changes, cochineal dyed textiles should only be cleaned with a neutral detergent to avoid inadvertent or undesired color changes.

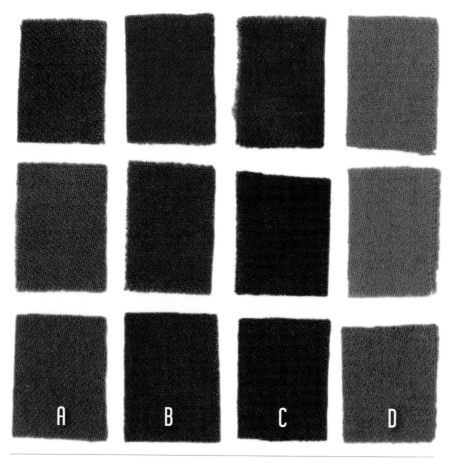

Cochineal on wool. Top row: alum pre-mordant, middle row: no pre-mordant, bottom row: no pre-mordant, treated with an iron post-mordant. The purples obtained from the iron post-mordant are very stable. Additions to dye bath include A. none, B. cream of tartar, C. citric acid, D. tin + cream of tartar.

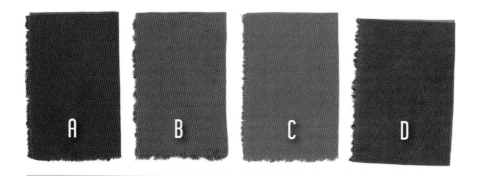

Cochineal dye on alum mordanted silk. Additions to dye bath: A. none, B. cream of tartar, C. tin + cream of tartar, D. no addition to dye bath / ferrous acetate post-mordant.

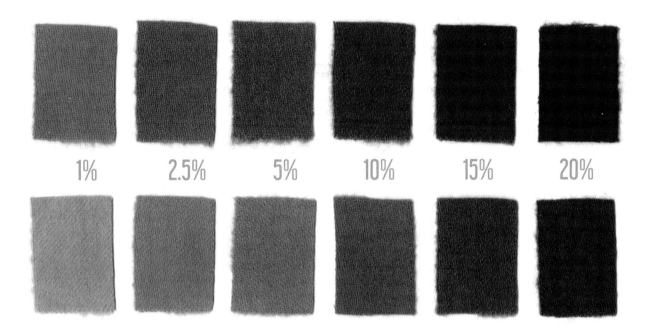

Cochineal on aluminum-mordanted wool at 1%, 2.5%, 5%, 10%, 15%, 20% w.o.f. Top: cream of tartar in dye bath, bottom: no cream of tartar.

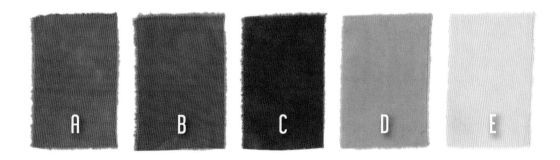

Cochineal on aluminum-mordanted cotton: A. no addition to dye bath, B. vinegar in dye bath, C. iron post-mordant, D. cream of tartar in dye bath, E. citric acid in dye bath. The high acidity of the cream of tartar and citric acid discharged the mordant from the cellulose textiles.

Dyes

Lac (*Laccifer lacca* or *Kerria lacca*)

Source: The dye is secreted by the female insect, which is enveloped in a resinlike substance and deposited on the branches of a host tree. The resin-coated branches are referred to as sticklac. The dye is contained in the secretions and must be removed from the resin, which is the source of lacquer (shellac). It is native to India, Southeast Asia, and China. Lac is usually available in easy-to-dissolve extract form. It is rarely available in its raw, resinous form outside the region where it is grown.

Chemical group: Anthraquinoid

Primary dyestuff: Laccaic acid

Class of dye: Lac is a mordant dye and is used for dyeing both protein and cellulose fibers.

Colors obtained: Crimson reds and burgundy if mordanted with aluminum, and purples when post-treated with iron.

Amount of dye: 5–12% w.o.f. lac extract

Extraction: If lac is obtained in raw form, the dye is extracted by boiling in a strong vinegar/water solution to release the dye from the resin. Continue to cook until the resin is almost clear. Strain the resinous clumps from the liquid dye.

Dyeing: Like cochineal, lac is pH sensitive, and the color may be shifted with the addition of acids or alkaline to the dye bath. The numerous dyes in lac are combined with sugars or proteins, and the addition of acids to the dye bath may help release the dyes from the sugars and shift the hue. Do not use acids when dyeing mordanted cellulose.

Lac extract on aluminum-mordanted wool: A. no addition to dye bath, B. citric acid added to dye bath.

Lac extract on aluminum-mordanted silk: A. no addition to dye bath, B. 1% iron post-mordant.

Lac extract on aluminum-mordanted cotton yarn: A. no addition to dye bath, B. 1% iron post-mordant.

Madder (*Rubia tinctorium*, *Rubia cordifolia*)

Source:	The dye develops in the roots of the plant, which are usually harvested after at least 3 years of growth. Once harvested, the roots are dried, which further develops the dye. Dyeing with fresh roots produces an inferior color compared to dyeing with dried roots. There are many varieties of madder, and each of these contains many different dyes. European madder (*Rubia tinctorium*) and Indian madder (*Rubia cordifolia*) are the primary commercial sources. Madder grows well in calcareous soil.
Chemical group:	Anthraquinoid
Primary dyestuff:	Alizarin is the primary red dye in *Rubia tinctorium*. Munjistin is the primary dye in *Rubia cordifolia*. Madder also contains purpurin, pseudopururin, and other dyes.
Class of dye:	Madder is a mordant dye and can be used to dye both protein and cellulose fibers.
Colors obtained:	Red with aluminum; purples and brown with iron. *Rubia tinctorium* contains more alizarin and produces Turkey red colors, while *Rubia cordifolia* is more orange in color, unless extracted by boiling with acid.
Amount of dye:	5–10% w.o.f. madder extract 25–200% w.o.f. dried roots

Extraction: Grind the dry madder roots as finely as possible. If using whole or chopped madder roots, soak the roots overnight. After soaking, the roots can be more finely ground by using a blender.

Cook ground *Rubia tinctorium* roots at a moderate temperature (maximum temperature 65°C/150°F) for at least 2 hours to completely extract the dye. Strain the liquid. Multiple extractions will likely release more dye from the roots.

To extract munjistin from *Rubia cordifolia*, add vinegar or citric acid to obtain a pH 4, and boil for 1 hour. After extraction, neutralize the dye solution with a small amount of soda ash before dyeing.

Dyeing: Add the textile to the bath and very slowly bring the temperature of the dye bath to 65°C/150ºF. Maintain that temperature for 1 hour.

Rubia tinctorium produces the clearest reds by using an aluminum mordant, and violets by using an iron mordant in hard water that contains calcium. If using soft water, add a small amount of calcium carbonate to the dye bath (approximately 1 grams per liter [g/L] of dye bath).

Other uses: Once the dye has been thoroughly extracted, the ground madder roots and the exhausted dye bath can be used as a reduction source for an indigo vat. Although the roots no longer contain dye, they do contain reducing sugars. *Rubia cordifolia* is used medicinally but *Rubia tinctorium* is not, because its high alizarin content is not safe for consumption. There are many other varieties of madder, each containing different combinations of dyes.

 CAUTION: Overheating *Rubia tinctorium* changes some of the dyes and releases anthragallol, resulting in browner tones.

Chapter 3
Dyes

	Alizarin	Munjistin	Anthragallol	Purpurin	Pseudopurpurin
THE MOST IMPORTANT DYES FOUND IN DIFFERENT TYPES OF MADDER					
Rubia tinctorium European Madder	x	x	x	x	x
Rubia cordifolia Indian Madder	x	x		x	x
Rubia peregrina Wild Madder	x			x	x
Galium verum Lady's Bedstraw	x			x	x
Rubia Akane Japanese Madder				x	x

Schweppe p. 231

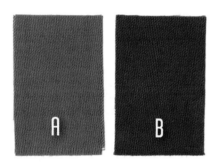

A. *Rubia cordifolia*, ground roots, boiled at pH 4 to extract munjistin. B. *Rubia cordifolia*, ground roots, low temperature extraction, no acid. Both dyed on aluminum-mordanted wool. The same madder roots can produce different colors, emphasizing different dyes, depending on the extraction method.

WOOL   SILK   COTTON

Top: madder roots (*Rubia tinctorium*), and bottom: madder extract (*Rubia cordifolia*) on aluminum-mordanted wool (left), silk (center), and cotton (right).

YELLOW DYES

Sources for yellow dyes most often contain flavonoids. Some contain both flavonoids and tannins. The flavonoids are released from the plant first, resulting in yellow colors. As the plant material cooks longer, tannins are released and are usually darker in color. The brightest, clearest yellows will attach to the textile early in the dyeing process, and the tannins will attach later.

Henna (*Lawsonia inermis*)

Source:	The dye comes from the leaves of the shrub or small tree. The plant is native to India.
Chemical group:	Naphthaquinoid
Primary dyestuffs:	Lawsone, luteolin, tannin
Class of dye:	Henna's lawsone is an oxidation dye and will dye wool without a mordant. The luteolin is a flavonoid and a mordant dye for both protein and cellulose fibers.
Colors obtained:	Yellows to orange browns on wool, and dull yellows on cellulose and silk when used as a mordant dye.
Amount of dye:	20–50% w.o.f. ground henna leaf powder

Extraction: Henna is usually available in the form of dry, very finely ground leaves. It may be placed in the dye bath along with the textile, or it may be cooked to extract the dye and then filtered to remove plant particles.

Dyeing: The luteolin, a yellow flavonoid, will attach to protein fibers first if there is a mordant present. Long dye baths will extract the darker shades of the lawsone. Add vinegar to the dye bath to shift the color toward orange.

Other uses: Henna was historically used to stimulate fermentation of indigo vats and is still used as a reduction material for the organic indigo vats. Precursors for lawsone are present in the plant. As these precursors oxidize into lawsone, the indigo is reduced. The plant also contains sugars useful for the reduction. The plant material may be used for immersion dyeing prior to its use in the indigo vat. In nontextile applications, it is commonly used as a hair dye and a temporary skin dye.

Dyes

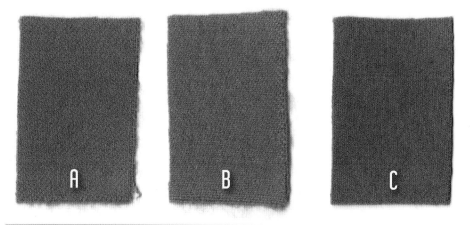

Henna, ground plant material @ 50% w.o.f. on wool: A. no mordant, B. no mordant, vinegar in dye bath, C. aluminum mordant. The flavonoids present in the dye attach only when there is a mordant, and will result in a stronger yellow color.

Henna applied to aluminum-mordanted silk.

Henna on aluminum-mordanted cotton yarn, and with a 1% iron post-mordant.

Myrobalan (*Terminalia chebula*)

Source: The dye is sourced from the nuts of the myrobalan tree.
Chemical groups: Tannin and flavonoid
Primary dyestuff: Flavonoid
Class of dye: Mordant dye
Colors obtained: Light yellow
Amount of dye: 2–10% w.o.f. extract
20–30% w.o.f. ground nuts when used as a dye
10–20% w.o.f. ground nuts when used as tannin prior to cellulose mordanting

Extraction: The finely ground nuts do not require any special extraction methods and may be put into the tannin bath or dye bath along with the textile.

Dyeing: Myrobalan is most often used as an excellent source of tannin. Nearly all cotton textiles in India are treated with myrobalan before mordanting. It is also the source of a pale-yellow dye that is very resistant to washing and light. Delicate greens can be achieved when myrobalan is combined with light shades of indigo.

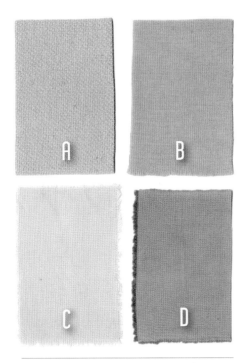

Myrobalan applied to aluminum-mordanted:
A. wool broadcloth, B. wool knit, C. silk,
D. silk with 1% ferrous acetate post-mordant.

Myrobalan on aluminum-mordanted cotton yarn (left) and with a 1% iron post-mordant (right). The dark gray of the iron-treated yarn indicates the presence of a large amount of tannin.

Dyes

Pomegranate (*Punica granatum*)

Source:	The rind of the fruit
Chemical group:	Flavonoid and tannin
Primary dyestuff:	Granatonine
Class of dye:	Mordant dye
Colors obtained:	Soft gold yellows with alum, and grays and greens with iron.
Amount of dye:	5–8% w.o.f. pomegranate extract
	100–200% w.o.f. ground pomegranate rind

Extraction: Pulverize dried pomegranate rinds as finely as possible. Soak the pulverized rinds for several hours, then simmer to extract the dye.

Dyeing: Pomegranate is an excellent source of tannin and also a dye. Lower temperatures and shorter dye baths will result in yellow tones from the flavonoids. Higher temperatures and longer dye times will develop the deeper gold/brown colors of the tannin.

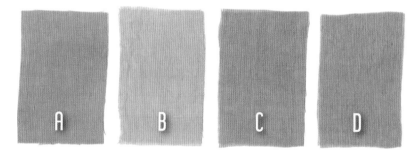

Pomegranate applied to aluminum-mordanted ramie: A. dried pomegranate rind at 100% w.o.f.; B., C., D. pomegranate extracts from various sources at 8% w.o.f.

Pomegranate applied to aluminum-mordanted wool and silk.

Pomegranate applied to aluminum-mordanted cotton yarn, using a 1% iron post-mordant.

Rhubarb
(*Rheum officinale*, *Rheum australe*, *Rheum x hybridum*, *Rheum rhabarbarum*, and others)

Source: The dye comes from the roots of plants that are several years old. The plant originated in Asia, but varieties are now grown around the world. Common garden rhubarb (*Rheum rhabarbarum*) is also a source of dye, and the information below applies to it. Rhubarb is the primary source of yellow on protein fibers when using the one-bath acid dye process.

Chemical group: Anthraquinoid and tannin

Primary dyestuff: Emodin and chrysophanol

Class of Dye: Mordant dye

Colors obtained: Bright yellow to yellow browns

Amount of dye: 2–5% w.o.f. extract
20–50% w.o.f. dried, powdered root
100–200% w.o.f. fresh root

Extraction: If using fresh or dried whole roots, chop them as finely as possible. Soak the roots for several hours or overnight, then simmer to extract the dye. If using finely powdered roots, they may be placed in the dye bath along with the textile, but a more even dyeing will result if the dye is extracted from the fine-powdered root and the extraction is filtered.

Rhubarb on aluminum-mordanted wool (A.), silk (B.), ramie (C.), hemp (D.).

Rhubarb applied to aluminum-mordanted cotton yarn, and with a 1% iron post-mordant.

Dyes

Weld (*Reseda luteola*)

Source: The dye is obtained from the leaves, flower heads, and small stems of the plant. It is native to southern Europe and is easily grown from seed in temperate climates.

Chemical group: Flavonoid

Primary dyestuff: Luteolin

Class of dye: Weld is a mordant dye and is used for dyeing both protein and cellulose fibers.

Colors obtained: Brilliant clear yellow with aluminum, and olive greens with iron

Amount of dye: 3–5% w.o.f. weld extract
50% w.o.f. dry plants
100–300% w.o.f. fresh plants

Extraction: Boil fresh or dried weld plant for 30 to 60 minutes. Strain.

Dyeing: Weld is one of the most important yellow dyes. It produces the clearest yellows in hard, calcareous water. If using soft water, add a small amount of calcium carbonate/chalk (approximately 1 g/L of dye bath) to brighten the color.

There are many additional flavonoids used for dyeing. Some of these are listed in the appendix, along with their respective lightfastness tests.

Aluminum-mordanted wool: A. no dye, B. wool dyed with weld, C. wool dyed with weld and chalk added to the dye bath. Chalk is not always necessary. The need to use chalk depends on the water and the processing of the wool.

Weld on aluminum-mordanted silk.

Weld on aluminum-mordanted cotton yarn, and with a 1% iron post-mordant.

BROWN DYES

Dyes that produce rich brown shades often require long, slow dye baths. Some contain large amounts of tannin. They are often combined with small amounts of iron to achieve deeper shades.

Black Walnut (*Juglans nigra*)

Source: Black walnut trees are native to eastern North America. The most concentrated dye is extracted from the outer husks/hulls of the walnuts. Use fresh hulls, freeze them, or dry them carefully for future use. Fresh or frozen walnut hulls contain a greater amount of soluble dye than dried walnuts. Gather walnuts with green husks, rather than those that have darkened and begun to rot on the ground. As the husks rot, the juglone is damaged, reacting with itself and forming an insoluble pigment. The leaves, bark, and wood also contain dye. Walnut extracts typically produce much-paler colors than fresh, frozen, or dried walnut husks.

Chemical group: Naphthaquinoid

Primary dyestuff: The husks contain juglone and a small amount of tannin. The leaves contain various flavonoids and tannins

Class of dye: Black walnut husks will dye directly on protein without a mordant and are a mordant dye on protein and cellulose. Black walnut leaves are a mordant dye.

Colors obtained: Deep greenish browns and gray brown with iron

Amount of dye: One fresh or frozen walnut husk per 20–25 g of fiber.
Two dried walnut husks for the same weight of fiber.
300–400% w.o.f. fresh leaves
100% w.o.f. dried leaves
25–50% w.o.f. extract

Extraction from husks: Place fresh or dry walnuts in a net bag and cover with water. Simmer the walnuts slowly for an hour or two. The husks will break down and separate from the nut hull inside (unless it had been removed already). Cool the bath to room temperature before adding the textile. Leave the husk material in the dye bath, since the dye will continue to be extracted.

Extraction from leaves: Cover fresh or dried leaves with water and boil for approximately 30 minutes. Strain.

Dyeing: A 1-hour walnut husk dye bath results in tan and light-brown colors. Long, slow dye baths of at least 4 hours produce the deepest brown shades. During the dye bath, the dye forms insoluble pigments inside the fiber. When dyeing with leaves, the flavonoids will attach to the textile first, and then the tannins will attach as it remains in the dye bath.

Chapter 3
Dyes

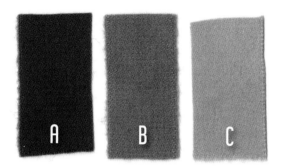

Black walnut husks dyed directly (no mordant) on wool: A. fresh walnut hulls, B. dried walnut hulls, C. walnut extract.

Black walnut leaves on aluminum-mordanted wool, and with 1% iron post-mordant.

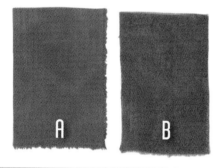

Black walnut hulls on silk: A. unmordanted, B. aluminum mordanted.

Black walnut leaves on aluminum-mordanted silk, and with 1% ferrous acetate post-mordant.

Black walnut hulls on aluminum-mordanted cotton yarn, and with 1% iron post-mordant.

Black walnut leaves on aluminum-mordanted cotton yarn, and with 1% iron post-mordant.

44

Cutch (*Acacia catechu*)

Source: The dye is extracted from the heartwood of an acacia tree that is native to India, Pakistan, and Nepal. The heartwood is boiled in water and the decoction is evaporated, resulting in cutch extract. Cutch can be found in either a crystallized or powder extract. The crystallized form is more difficult to dissolve and should be soaked for several hours in water before use.

Chemical group: Flavonoid and condensed tannin

Primary dyestuff: Cathechin

Class of dye: Cutch dyes directly on protein without a mordant, binding by affinity (molecular attraction) and electrical attraction as an acid dye. It is a mordant dye on protein and cellulose.

Colors obtained: Cinnamon browns with aluminum, and deep browns with iron

Amount of Dye: 5–50% w.o.f. extract.

Cutch is always purchased in the form of an extract, but the strength of that extract varies widely. Consult with your supplier or do tests to determine the dye strength.

Dyeing: Cutch performs best with a long, slow, heated dye bath and is effective on both protein and cellulose fibers.

Cutch: A. on wool, no mordant, B. alum-mordanted wool, C. alum-mordanted silk, D. alum-mordanted linen.

Cutch on alum-mordanted cotton yarn, and with 1% iron post-mordant.

 NOTE: Tannins will attach to a wool textile without mordant, but flavonoids will attach only if mordant is used, resulting in a more yellow tone of the wool.

Dyes

TANNINS

Tannins are found in barks, wood, seedpods, nuts, or leaves and can often be sourced from local environments. Some plants contain better-quality or more concentrated amounts of tannin. The root of the word "tannin" can also be seen in "tanin" (French for tannin), "tannenbaum," the Old High German word for oak or fir tree, and the medieval Latin "tannare," which means "to convert to leather."

Tannins are weak acids and are somewhat astringent, causing a dry puckering sensation in the mouth when ingested. This can be experienced when drinking young red wines that have not yet aged and mellowed over time. When tannins are applied topically, they dry out the skin—a good reason to wear gloves if immersing the hands in a tannin bath. This unpleasant astringency helps protect the plant from insects or other predators. The astringent quality of tannins has long been at the heart of the leather-tanning industry, where tannins change the nature of animal hide proteins, making them resistant to bacteria and rot and producing soft leather.

Tannins are a very important component in the natural dye process due to their role in mordanting. They are water soluble and are easily extracted in warm water. Tannins have an affinity for both protein and cellulose fibers. When tannins are combined with mordants, they form mineral tannates, which are insoluble compounds. Formation of the tannin/mordant compound is crucial to the mordanting of cellulose. When tannin is combined with any amount of iron, a gray or black color will result.

Since cellulose fibers do not bind readily with mordants, tannin is applied as a first step in the immersion-mordanting process. Once the mordant is applied, the tannin loses its solubility and forms a very strong bond with the mordant inside the textile. In Turkey red printing, this step is called "galling" or "sumaching," referring to the type of tannin used.

All tannins, when used as a dye source, are resistant to fading. In fact, tannins tend to darken after lengthy exposure to light. When used in combination with other dyes, tannins can improve the lightfastness of those dyes. Tannins do this by protecting the natural colors from UV light, mirroring their role of protecting the plant from UV light. Some tannin-based plants also contain flavonoids or other dyes. The flavonoids may fade when exposed to light, but the tannin remains. On protein fibers, some tannins are used as sources of color, either with or without mordants. A mordant is always required with cellulose fibers.

There are three major classes of tannins:

Gallic Tannins

These are basically colorless. They are valuable in assisting the attachment of mordants to cellulose fibers and as a UV protectant on both protein and cellulose fibers. These tannins react strongly to the presence of iron, producing gray and black tones whenever they are combined with ferrous sulfate or ferrous acetate. This is an important effect that is regularly used in cotton printing. The most common sources of gallic tannins for the dyer include oak gall, sumac, and tara.

Oak galls (gallnuts) are one of the richest sources of tannin. They are growths of plant tissue produced by an oak tree in reaction to insect-released chemicals. The galls are found on a variety of oak trees around the world. The Aleppo oak (*Quercus infectoria*) produces some of the most tannin-concentrated galls. Native to western Asia and eastern Europe, they are a source of some medicines and commercial tannin.

Staghorn sumac (*Rhus typhina*) and smooth sumac (*Rhus glabra*) grow wild throughout North America. The tannin is present in the leaves, bark, and roots. Leaves

 CAUTION: Poison sumac (*Toxicodendron vernix*) is not a source of tannin and should be avoided.

can be collected and dried in the fall and can be used throughout the year as a source of tannin.

Tara comes from the pods of a small shrub (*Caesapinia spinosa*) that is native to Peru.

Ellagic Tannins

These tannins also contain yellow colorants (flavonoids) and are frequently used as a source of yellow dye. Their tannin content is high and they are used to attach mordants to cellulose. Common ellagic tannins include myrobalan and pomegranate rind.

Myrobalan is commonly applied to cotton textiles in India prior to mordanting or printing.

Condensed Tannins

All condensed tannins are reddish or brownish. In general, they are a weaker source of tannin and do not react as strongly to iron mordants as the gallic and ellagic tannins. They can be used directly on protein fibers or as a mordant dye on protein and cellulose. Cutch and quebracho are the most widely used examples of condensed tannin. Also within this category are black teas and chestnut bark. Condensed tannins oxidize when exposed to light, increasing their red or brown tones. Treatment with an alkali, during or after dyeing, darkens the colors and brings out the red tones, but these colors tend to be less resistant to light than those obtained without the use of the alkali.

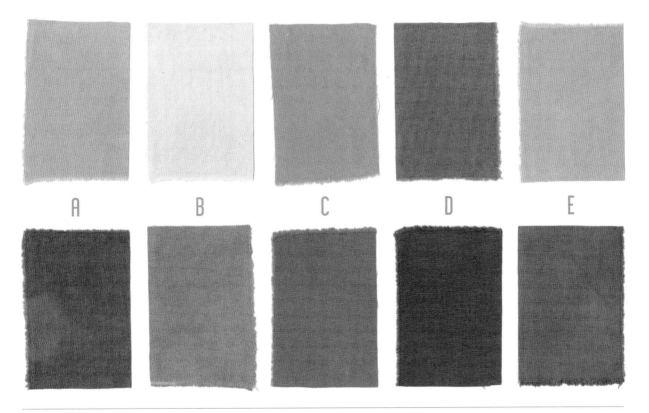

Ellagic (yellow) tannins and condensed (red) tannins used as dyes on aluminum-mordanted cotton (top row) and with 1% iron post-mordant (bottom row): A. pomegranate, B. myrobalan, C. quebracho, D. cutch, E. chestnut. The ellagic tannins produce green shades when treated with iron, while the condensed tannins are browner.

Chapter 3
Dyes

Tannic acid is a commercial form of tannin. It is produced for the leather-tanning industry by hydrolyzing gallic or ellagic tannins, which means that they are split with water into sugars and tannic acid.

Tannic acid often contains condensed tannins as well, which might impart red colors. Tannic acid can be used in the dyeing/mordanting process but is often a weaker source of tannin than those in their original form, which are still bound to the sugars (e.g., gallnut, myrobalan, sumac). Condensed tannins cannot be hydrolyzed and contain no tannic acid.

BLUE DYE

Indigo is the primary source of blue dye for natural dyers. The dye is classified as an indigoid dye, technically named indigotin but here referred to generally as "indigo." It can be sourced from the leaves of several different plants and has a history of cultivation and use on nearly every continent. The leaves of the plants contain only the precursors of indigo.

Additionally, all indigo contains certain amounts of indirubin, an isomer of indigo that reduces in the same way as indigo. Indirubin is a red dye that is present in varying amounts, resulting in some indigo blues that are more purplish than others. The process's variables, such as extraction method, storage, and temperature, can influence the amount of indirubin present.

The most common method of extracting indigo from plants is by using a water soak method. The insoluble pigment is then precipitated and usually dried into cakes or powder, which are easy to store and transport. Once extracted, the precursors are converted into soluble leuco (colorless) indigo by using fermentation in the vat (see "Indigo Reduction" on page 73). Extraction can also be accomplished by composting the plant material. This process concentrates the indigo in the form of *sukumo* (Japan) or woad balls (Europe). In addition to the dye pigment, these forms also contain organic material and microorganisms (bacteria) that are used to start the fermentation of the vat.

The extraction and dye process for indigo is more complex than for other natural dyes and is the source of ritual, legend, and lore. Worldwide, there are hundreds of plants that produce indigo. Some of the most common plants are listed below:

- *Indigofera tinctoria* is grown in India and has a high concentration of the indigo precursors. It requires a hot growing season. It was grown commercially on the southern coast of South Carolina in the eighteenth century. Most natural indigo that is sold commercially is this variety.

- *Indigofera guatemalensis* and *Indigofera suffruticosa* are South American varieties of indigo. These were important plants for local use in Central America and as an export crop in the eighteenth century. They are still being grown today, mostly for local use.

- *Isatis tinctoria*, also known as woad, is the European source of blue dye. It contains fewer indigo precursors than other commercial varieties, resulting in lighter colors. The precursors in woad are different from those in other indigo plants.

- *Persicaria tinctoria* is also known as Japanese indigo or dyer's knotweed. It grows well in temperate zones and is commonly used in the making of *sukumo*, but the pigment can also be extracted by a water soak method.

Synthetic indigo is molecularly identical to natural indigo and can be used in any of the indigo vats, but its production is through a chemical process and is a source of industrial pollution. Once applied to the fibers it is impossible to discern the difference between "natural" and "synthetic" indigo.

Although indigo may be used as a dye from fresh leaves or from composted leaves, within the scope of this book "indigo" refers to the use of extracted and dried indigo pigment.

USING LOCAL DYES

Many dyers prefer to use plants foraged from their local environment. This can be cost effective, as well as a reflection of place, provided they are dyes of good quality. Care must always be taken not to gather rare or endangered species.

The best plants that we can gather for dyeing (leaves, roots, barks, stems, pods, and some flowers) contain either flavonoids or tannins. Many contain both. Carotenoids (a chemical group), on the other hand, are ineffective as textile dyes since they are soluble in oils and fats and insoluble in water. Additionally, they are unstable when exposed to light and heat. Carotenoids are the source of yellow, orange, and red pigments, often found in edible plants and flowers (such as carrots, pumpkin, and California poppies). Chlorophyll, a source of green in many plants, is also unstable as a dye. Anthocyanins (a chemical group) are present in most purple, red, or blue flowers and plants (such as red cabbage). They are not stable to pH changes and are not considered effective textile dyes.

Anthraquinoid dyes, the types of red dyes found in cultivated madder root, are more rare and seldom found in foraged wild plants other than the fine roots of wild madder or the bark of the buckthorn (rhamnus species). Indigo is the only true source of blue and rarely grows wild.

To learn more about the foraged plant material's constituents to predict how useful they may be for dye, here are some quick tests that can be used. Research or more elaborate testing would be needed to identify the exact nature of these components, but for your needs, that may not be as important as objective observation.

Test for flavonoids:

- Dye two wool textiles: one that has been pre-mordanted with alum and one that has not. If color attaches without a mordant, then there may be dyes present that can be applied directly. If the color obtained is brighter or more yellow on the mordanted textile, the dye likely contains flavonoids, which will only attach when a mordant is present.

Test for tannin:

- Place a textile that has been dyed with the foraged plant material (any fiber, with or without aluminum mordant) in a bath with 1 percent w.o.f. iron mordant. Tannins react to iron and will turn dark on contact. A light gray will result if there is a small amount of tannin; a darker shade, if the tannin is strong. When flavonoid dyes are present and aluminum mordant has been used prior to the dyeing, the resulting color will be green when treated with the iron mordant.

Test the dye for stability and longevity:

- Once the dyeing is complete, the dye should be well attached to the fibers, and the textile should rinse clear with little or no dye in the rinse water. This applies to mordant dyes and those applied directly without a mordant. Evaluate the dyed textile by using lightfast tests as described in chapter 10.

Dyes

Most foraged plants will produce yellow, tan, or brown colors. Plants gathered at different times of the year may produce varying quantities of colorants and tannins. Foraged dye plants may require more dyestuff per weight of textile than the classical dyes. The use of additional dye plants, either grown or purchased, may be necessary to achieve a full palette of color, including the reds and indigo blue.

Care should be taken when gathering any dye plant in the wild. Learn to positively identify known dye plants. Do not remove bark from live trees or denude a plant of all its foliage. Bark can be foraged from recently felled saplings or trees early in the spring, when the sap is running. Avoid rare or endangered plants and never gather in protected areas such as national parks or national forests. Always leave behind more than you harvest. Investigate invasive species as potential dye sources. Consult with local, experienced dyers and, if possible, grow and harvest your own plants for the greatest sustainability.

CHAPTER 4
Mordants

An understanding of mordant substances is vital in order to use natural dyes successfully. This chapter defines the various mordants to help the dyer navigate between the available choices. Chemicals that are used to assist in the mordanting process will also be described. Application of the mordants is discussed in later chapters.

A mordant is a metal salt that is used to fix a dye in the fiber. The mordant binds to the fiber (protein) or is left as an insoluble compound on the fiber (cellulose), and the dye binds to the mordant. The word comes from the French word *mordre*, which means "to bite." The mordant "bites" the tongue when tasted, which was a common approach to testing chemicals in earlier times but is not recommended as a method today. The quality, quantity, and application of the mordant will affect the final color of the dye. The mordant is essential for the lightfastness and washfastness of a mordant dye.

A small amount of mordant will produce a pale color, while the use of a greater amount of mordant will allow more dye to attach, resulting in a stronger color. The goal is to have enough mordant in the fiber to allow the maximum amount of color. Lighter colors are best achieved by using less dye, not less mordant, since the dyes are usually the more costly ingredient. Once the mordant is bound to the dye, it is no longer available to bind with additional dye. If the textile will be overdyed, then it is helpful to apply more than the minimum amount of mordant to the textile. Too much of any mordant can be damaging to the fiber.

Historically, dyers often placed the mordant, dye, and fiber in the dye pot at the same time. This approach saved fuel, water, and time. Today, mordant is rarely put directly into the dye bath, since we understand that it is not the best practice and does not maximize the process. If mordant and dye are put into the dye pot together, they bind into an insoluble compound before either one effectively penetrates into the textile. For this reason, mordanting and dyeing is normally a two-step process.

Once a mordant has been properly applied to a textile, it is stable and ready to accept dye. The textile can be dyed immediately or dried for future dyeing.

NONE   2%   5%   10%   15%   20%

Dyes: weld and madder. The samples show that increasing the amount of aluminum on silk (from no mordant to 20% w.o.f.) results in an increase in the amount of dye that is able to attach to the textile. Although there is little visible increase in dye color beyond 10%, surplus mordant in the textile is helpful to bind additional dye when overdyeing.

Mordants

Mordanted textiles that have been dried may require a longer time to wet out than nonmordanted textiles.

When purchasing mordants and mordant assists (see page 56) from chemical and dye suppliers, ask for them by their proper scientific name. Material Safety Data Sheets (MSDS) should be available to help verify chemical formulas and names to ensure accuracy. Important: Always use fresh chemicals for the best results.

Aluminum

The most commonly used mordants are a variety of chemical salts made from aluminum. They are inexpensive, relatively safe to use, and produce the purest color from the dye. They have a long history of use around the world as mordants and in other applications, such as water purification, blood coagulants, deodorants, and treating animal hides to make parchment. Aluminum is the active ingredient in all forms of aluminum salts.

There are several different types of aluminum mordants, and it is essential to understand the differences in order to choose the correct mordant and the amount of that mordant. Each aluminum salt contains differing amounts of aluminum. For instance, only three-quarters the amount of aluminum sulfate is required to achieve the same performance of potassium aluminum sulfate dodecahydrate (alum). The quantities required of each can be calculated by using the molecular weights of each mordant (refer to molecular weights in the appendix).

POTASSIUM ALUMINUM SULFATE DODECAHYDRATE (ALUM)

Potassium aluminum sulfate dodecahydrate [$KAl(SO_4)_2 \cdot 12H_2O$] is the most widely available mordant. It is used to mordant protein fibers and is also used to make neutral aluminum acetate. When combined with a soda ash solution, it becomes a mordant for cellulose. This is a crystallized form of alum and includes twelve molecules of water. It is often referred to as potassium alum, potash alum, or simply "alum." Alum was traditionally mined as a ground mineral. It can still be located naturally in several places around the world, but most alum is now industrially produced. This manufactured mordant is ordinarily very clean, meaning that it contains no iron, which would dull the color. All future references to "alum" in this book refer to potassium aluminum sulfate dodecahydrate.

ALUMINUM SULFATE

Aluminum sulfate [$Al_2(SO_4)_3$] can also be used to mordant protein. It is inexpensive, readily available, and often used in the craft of marbling. It does not occur naturally and is always manufactured. In the past, it was considered an inferior mordant because it contained a considerable amount of iron. Today it is produced by using a different process and is usually free of iron. It is always a good idea to test this mordant before use to ensure the absence of iron. Aluminum sulfate contains more aluminum than alum.

AMMONIUM ALUMINUM SULFATE

Ammonium aluminum sulfate (pickling alum) [$(NH_4)Al(SO_4)_2$] can also be used to successfully mordant protein fiber. It is typically packaged and sold in small quantities in the grocery store, making it an expensive product for use in the dye kitchen.

POTASSIUM ALUMINUM SULFATE

Potassium aluminum sulfate [$KAl(SO_4)_2$] is a water-free alum, also called calcinated or burnt alum. This refers to the fact that it has been heated to a high temperature in order to evaporate the water molecules. Burnt alum is most commonly used in Japan and is stronger, but somewhat harder to dissolve, than alum. It is not readily available in the United States.

ALUMINUM ACETATE

Aluminum acetate is an aluminum salt of acetic acid. It is a mordant for cellulose. It is primarily used for printing but can also be applied as a mordant for immersion dyeing on any cellulose textile. Although it can be used to mordant silk, the less expensive alum is equally effective. Aluminum acetate is available in different forms:

- Neutral aluminum acetate (also referred to as aluminum triacetate) [$Al(CH_3CO_2)_3$]
- Monobasic aluminum acetate (also referred to as aluminum diacetate) [$Al(OH)(CH_3CO_2)_2$]
- Dibasic aluminum acetate (also referred to as basic aluminum monoacetate) [$Al(OH)_2 CH_3CO_2$]

All three forms of aluminum acetate work equally well. The neutral aluminum triacetate is the most stable form but is difficult to purchase in that form. It can be made directly from alum, when needed, and that is the approach that we recommend. The recipe is included in chapter 11.

Most suppliers carry either monobasic aluminum acetate or dibasic aluminum acetates. Both of these have a limited shelf life, so it is important to work with fresh mordants. Monobasic aluminum acetate and dibasic aluminum acetate contain more aluminum, per weight unit, than the neutral aluminum acetate.

 CAUTION: Monobasic and dibasic aluminum acetate mordants are in the form of very lightweight powders that can easily become airborne and irritate the throat and nasal passages. Always use a dust mask when handling these until they have been dissolved in water.

ALUMINUM FROM PLANTS

Some plants that grow in soil with a high concentration of aluminum are capable of absorbing the aluminum through their roots. These plants are called hyperaccumulators and include tea, camellia, club moss, and symplocos, among others. When the amount of aluminum that has been absorbed by the plant is sufficient, it can be extracted from the plant material by boiling in water to mordant textiles. The Bebali Foundation, in collaboration with Michel Garcia, has done significant research regarding the symplocos plant leaves used by the Indonesian dyers. The dyer who wishes to work with plant mordants can be assured that this is a sustainable product, and we can recommend it as an alternative to mineral alum. Most dyers will choose to use mineral alum because of its low cost and availability.

Mordants

Iron

Iron salts are used as mordants to "sadden" or darken colors. Iron will shift a yellow dye toward green and a pink dye toward purple. If combined with tannin it produces a gray or black. Small amounts of iron will improve the lightfastness of dyes.

Iron is seldom used as a primary mordant but is more often used in combination with aluminum or as a post-dye treatment to alter a color. Use only a small amount (1–2% of the textile weight). Too much iron will leave the fiber feeling harsh and susceptible to deterioration. Iron is used in two different forms: ferrous sulfate and ferrous acetate.

FERROUS SULFATE

Ferrous sulfate [$FeSO_4$] is the most common form of iron for the dyer. When iron is present in a textile, the damage caused to the fiber by oxygen and UV light is accelerated. Ferrous sulfate generates some sulfuric acid when dissolved, and it is harmful to any textile.

Ferrous sulfate may be used in small amounts with cotton or wool but is not recommended for silk. Silk is more sensitive to UV light than either wool or cellulose. As a result, silk textiles are more sensitive to damage from iron.

🌿 Refer to recipe 13.

FERROUS ACETATE

Iron (ferrous acetate) [$Fe(CH_3CO_2)_2$] is an iron salt of acetic acid. It is used in mordant printing and can also be used as a post-dye treatment to sadden the color on wool, silk, or cellulose fibers. Ferrous acetate is preferred over ferrous sulfate because it releases acetic acid, which evaporates quickly and causes less damage to the fiber than sulfuric acid, which is released from ferrous sulfate. Ferrous acetate is not readily available for purchase since its shelf life would be limited. The ferrous acetate mordant is easily made from ferrous sulfate and sodium acetate. Rusty nails, or other source of iron, when soaked in vinegar will produce ferrous acetate, but it is difficult to control the amount of iron in such a solution.

🌿 Refer to recipe 14.

Post-mordant baths of 2% ferrous acetate after dyeing with weld (silk) and madder (cotton). Time in post-mordant bath: 1 minute, 2 minutes, and 3 minutes.

Copper

Copper Sulfate [$CuSO_4$] is a metal salt that is usually used as a post mordant but sometimes used as a pre-mordant. Its effect on fiber is to sadden the color and turn it slightly "greenish." It will also improve lightfastness.

Copper requires care in handling and disposal. It is used as both an herbicide and a fungicide. The safest approach to working with copper, and the *only* one we recommend, is to leach the mineral from a copper or brass pot, or from small pieces of copper pipe in the dye pot. The very small amount of copper that is absorbed from the metal attaches to the dye in the fiber, eliminating the danger of disposing any copper in solution.

🌿 Refer to recipe 15.

Tin

Stannous chloride [$SnCl_2$] is a metal salt that will brighten some dye colors on wool or silk, (particularly cochineal red, which can be shifted to a scarlet hue). It can also be used to brighten yellows or turn madder a brilliant orange. Traditionally, tin was added directly to the dye bath but it can also be used as a pre-mordant instead of aluminum. Tin was not used in natural dyeing until the seventeenth century. Although it may have a reputation as being a "dangerous" mordant, it is actually no more toxic than aluminum or iron. Tin is far more expensive by weight than other mordants but only very small amounts are required, so in practice it is often affordable. Use it only when its special effects are desired or to achieve a color that cannot be achieved in any other way. An excess of tin can leave the fibers brittle and damaged. Cream of tartar is usually added to the bath to moderate the acidity of the tin mordant and to help keep the fiber soft.

🌿 Refer to recipe 7.

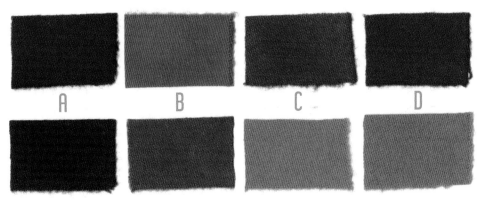

Color variations are obtained by using aluminum and tin mordants on wool, dyed with madder (top row) and cochineal (bottom row): A. aluminum pre-mordant, B. tin pre-mordant, C. tin and cream of tartar in dye bath, no pre-mordant, D. tin and cream of tartar in dye bath with alum pre-mordant.

Chrome

Potassium dichromate [$K_2Cr_2O_7$] is not recommended as a mordant or color enhancer, although it was used a great deal in the past. It is considered a health hazard and produces toxic waste.

Mordant Assists

Chemicals described as mordant assists are used to change the chemical structure of the mordant, to modify the pH, or to help fix the mordant on the textile.

CREAM OF TARTAR

Cream of tartar, *potassium tartrate* $[KC_4H_5O_6]$ is an acid salt that helps modify the pH of the wool mordant bath by lowering it slightly. Heated mordant baths can be harsh on wool and the pH adjustment helps protect the wool during the mordanting and gives it a better hand. It will also slow down the absorption of the mordant on wool, functioning as a leveling agent and resulting in more even dyeing.

Cream of tartar is not used when mordanting silk. Silk is mordanted without heat and dyed at lower temperatures so it is not subjected to the high temperature baths used with wool that might damage the fiber. Additionally, silk does not have the same tolerance for acidity as wool. The increased acidity from the cream of tartar would slow down the absorption of mordants too much and less of the mordant will be able to attach.

Cream of tartar is also useful in binding any small traces of iron, which might be in the water, resulting in clearer dye colors. Since iron has typically been removed in water treatment, most "city" water should not require cream of tartar to bind iron.

DUNG

Traditionally, cow dung was used to neutralize and fix mordants on cellulose fibers when tannins were not applied prior to the mordant. The phosphates and enzymes in the dried dung are the active ingredients. The enzymes are also useful in removing the gum thickeners from printed mordants. This process is called "dunging" and the term has continued to be used in the dye industry even when compounds other than real dung are used. Chalk (calcium carbonate) $[CaCO_3]$ is now used to neutralize and fix the mordant in situations where dung was traditionally used,. Sometimes it is combined with wheat bran, which contains enzymes that help to remove gums from mordants that have been thickened.

TANNIN

Tannin has an affinity for all fibers. Its affinity for cellulose is an important component of mordanting cellulose for immersion dyeing. When a cellulose textile is treated first with tannin, an insoluble compound will be formed when the textile is exposed to the mordant, fixing both in the fiber.

SODA ASH

Soda ash, sodium carbonate $[Na_2CO_3]$ is an alkaline substance that is used in combination with alum when making both aluminum acetate and an alum/soda ash mordant for cellulose.

SODIUM ACETATE

Sodium acetate $[CH_3CO_2Na]$ is the sodium salt of acetic acid and is used to make aluminum acetate and ferrous acetate.

CHAPTER 5
Immersion Dyeing

Immersion dyeing is defined as surrounding the textile with enough liquid to allow an even take-up of dye. Here we discuss the steps included in immersion dyeing, including mordanting and the actual dyeing process. Also included are alternative approaches to immersion dyeing, and how to recycle mordant and dye baths. Specific recipes for mordanting and other processes are found in Chapter 11.

Mordanting

Provided enough mordant is applied initially, no additional mordant will be necessary to over-dye a textile. When applied correctly, the mordant is fixed in the textile but it can be removed by a change in pH. Strong acids will remove the mordant. Strong alkali will damage the mordant.

All textiles must be rinsed thoroughly after mordanting to remove any unfixed mordant from the textile.

The presence of cream of tartar during the mordanting process will slow the absorption and level the distribution of the mordant in the textile. **Use cream of tartar only with wool.**

Silk is always mordanted without the use of heat, because the acidic mordant, if heated, can change the gloss and the hand of silk. Silk fibers are much thinner

MORDANTS FOR PROTEIN FIBERS

The amount of mordant required for immersion mordanting of protein can vary from 10-20% per weight of dry textile. This is dependent on the type of mordant used, the type of fiber, or the breed of sheep from which the wool is sourced.

Wool is most often mordanted in a heated bath. The heat swells the fiber, opens up the scales, and allows the mordant to penetrate inside the fiber. Without heat, the mordant process requires more time.

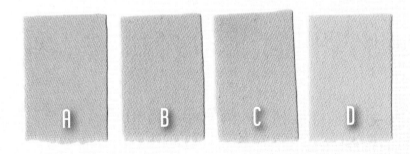

The use of slow, unheated mordant bath for wool: A. 24 hours in mordant bath, B. 2 days, C. 4 days, D. traditional heated mordant. The unheated mordant bath was made by using hot tap water (48°C/120°F), and no additional heat was applied. Dyed with weld.

Immersion Dyeing

than wool fibers and the absence of scales makes the penetration of the mordant easier. Cream of tartar is never used when mordanting silk because the increased acidity will cause less of the mordant to attach to the fiber.

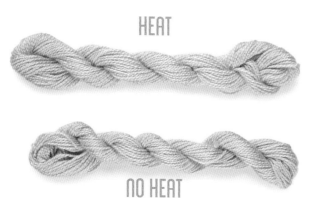

HEAT

NO HEAT

Silk yarn, mordanted: A. with heat, B. without heat, both dyed with weld. The unheated skein, in addition to being brighter in color, is also shinier and has a better "hand."

Alternatively, silk may be dyed and mordanted by using a "middle mordant" process, an approach practiced and refined in Japan. The textile is first immersed in the dye, then in the mordant, and then finished by returning the textile to the dye. This three-step process is an excellent approach to illustrate how dyes and mordants work.

This *dye-mordant-dye* sequence shows that the sequence of mordanting and dyeing is not always as important as the fact that both dye and mordant combine in the textile. This process works because silk absorbs mordants without heat, and dye can easily penetrate the fiber. This is the process used by Dr. Kazuki Yamazaki of Kusaki-Kobo Dye Studio (Japan), whose family has dyed silk in this way for three generations. They build deep, traditional colors on silk, often repeating the process by adding fresh dye and mordants.

🌿 Refer to recipes 5, 6, 7, 8, 9, and 10.

STEP 1

STEP 2

STEP 3

Middle mordant on silk fabric with cochineal dye. **Step 1**. First immersion in the dye bath, **Step 2**. Immersion in the mordant, **Step 3**. Returning the textile to the dye bath. The color deepens dramatically during the third step.

MORDANTS FOR CELLULOSE FIBERS

Cellulose fibers are a greater challenge to dye than protein fibers. There is no chemical affinity between the mordant and cellulose, and the mordant does not bind to the textile. There are two approaches that can be used to mordant cellulose.

- Tannin is used to fix the mordant in the fiber to achieve even, immersion dyeing.
- Without tannin, a concentrated solution of aluminum acetate is applied with a quick immersion, followed by drying and dunging.

All mordants for cellulose are cold mordant processes; the mordant bath is never heated. Heating the mordant solutions will damage the mordant, causing some of it to become insoluble and precipitate in the bath. As a result, less mordant will penetrate the textile.

Mordanting Cellulose with Tannin

Tannin has an affinity for cellulose fibers and will attach readily, though weakly, and can be removed with vigorous washing. When a textile is mordanted following the application of tannin, the bond between the tannin and mordant becomes stable and insoluble, fixing the mordant in the fiber. This method significantly improves the depth, evenness, and lightfastness of the color. Some older recipes for mordanting cellulose fibers repeat these steps several times, building up greater amounts of tannin, mordant, tannin, mordant. We have observed that a single application of tannin, followed by the mordant, is sufficient. Gallic tannins (gallnut, sumac, and tara) are the best choice for this pre-mordant tannin step. They are high in tannin content and provide good UV protection for the fibers and dye. They will result in the least alteration to the subsequent color of the dye. Ellagic tannins, such as myrobalan or pomegranate, can also be used but may cause alteration of the color.

Alum alone is not a suitable mordant for cellulose, and its use will produce inferior colors. Either aluminum acetate or alum combined with soda ash is recommended for mordanting cellulose. Early in the twentieth century the alum/soda ash recipe was used in industry because of its effectiveness and affordability. The soda ash reacts with the alum to make a compound that is similar to that used in Turkey red dyeing.

🌿 Refer to recipe 11.

Tannin and aluminum acetate mordant on cotton: A. unheated mordant application, B. heated mordant application. Heat damaged some of the mordant, preventing it from attaching to the textile.

Chapter 5
Immersion Dyeing

A   B   C   D   E   F

10% gallnut extract

10% sumac leaves

30% sumac leaves

10% myrobalan extract

10% pomegranate extract

10% tannic acid

The comparison of tannins, illustrated on page 60, shows the effect of various tannins and what happens at different steps of the tannin/mordant/dye process.

- A. The textile was first treated with the tannin. This is not a strong bond and must be fixed with a mordant.

- B. When immersed in an iron mordant, the tannin becomes insoluble and the color immediately turns dark. The depth of the gray color from the iron is a good indicator of the amount of tannin.

- C. Once treated with aluminum mordant, the tannin becomes stable and insoluble. The subtle color from any flavonoids present in the tannin becomes evident.

- D. When the aluminum-mordanted textile is immersed in an iron mordant, the effect of the iron is much less dramatic since most of the tannin sites are already bound to the aluminum. This is similar to what happens when dyed textiles are post-mordanted in iron.

- E and F. The samples were dyed in weld and madder. The amount of the tannin affects the amount of mordant bound to the textile and thus the depth of color when dyed.

Gallnut and myrobalan tannin baths were both made from concentrated extracts. The sumac tannin is ground plant material and not as concentrated. A level of 30 percent (w.o.f.) sumac is required to match the amount of tannin in 10 percent gall and myrobalan extracts. Tannin acid, often recommended for cellulose mordanting, has less tannin than gallnut or myrobalan extracts.

Mordanting Cellulose without Tannin

Cellulose can be mordanted without tannin, provided that a concentrated aluminum acetate solution is used. After the mordant is applied to the textile, it must be dried and then dunged, to complete fixation. This approach to mordanting is similar to the mordant printing methods described in chapter 8. It is more difficult to achieve an even application of dye and mordant with this method. However, it is a suitable approach for resisted fabrics or yarns such as *shibori* and ikat, where uniform dyeing is not so important. Tannins may be applied prior to this concentrated mordant. The tannin will improve the lightfastness and eliminate the need to dung the textile.

Refer to recipe 12·

OPPOSITE: Comparison of tannins, applied to cotton, treated with mordants, and dyed. The samples demonstrate the use of tannins for the mordanting of cellulose and what happens at each step.

Comparison of mordants on cotton: A. tannin, aluminum acetate, B. tannin, alum / soda ash, C. tannin, alum only, D. aluminum acetate, no tannin, E. alum / soda ash, no tannin, F. concentrated aluminum acetate, no tannin, dried and dunged.

Chapter 5
Immersion Dyeing

COMPARISON OF IMMERSION-MORDANTING SEQUENCES

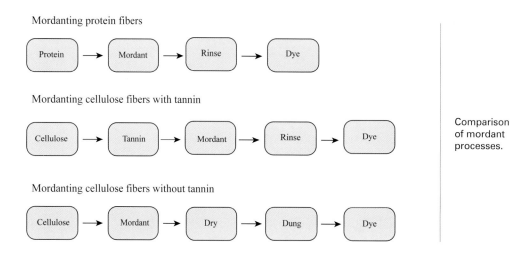

Mordanting protein fibers

Protein → Mordant → Rinse → Dye

Mordanting cellulose fibers with tannin

Cellulose → Tannin → Mordant → Rinse → Dye

Mordanting cellulose fibers without tannin

Cellulose → Mordant → Dry → Dung → Dye

Comparison of mordant processes.

Mordanting Multiple Fibers

The use of a different mordant process for each fiber (wool, silk, cellulose) ensures that all fibers absorb the maximum amount of mordant with the least damage to the fiber. Once mordanted, the different fibers may be dyed together in the same dye bath. Since the dye attaches to the mordant (not to the fiber), results will be very similar when the fibers are dyed together versus separately.

Textiles that are constructed from multiple fibers must be mordanted and dyed together. Consequently, different fiber types may not receive the optimum amount of mordant. Silk/wool combinations are all protein, but one fiber (wool or silk) will likely absorb more (or less) mordant, depending on the nature of the fiber.

Protein/cellulose combinations are commonly found in knitting yarns and in some textiles. There is no "right" way to approach the mordanting of these textiles. When

50% merino / 50% Tencel

50% superwash wool / 50% cotton

30% merino / 70% cotton

Yarns constructed of cellulose and wool. Comparison of mordants, dyed with madder: A. heated immersion mordant for wool, B. immersion mordant for cellulose with tannin.

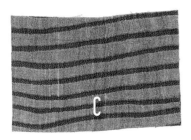

Fabric woven of linen and silk. Comparison of mordants, all dyed with cochineal: A. mordanted for cellulose with tannin, B. mordanted for protein/silk, C. mordanted for protein/silk, with cream of tartar added to the cochineal dye bath; the acid of the cream of tartar discharged the mordant that attached to the linen.

treated as cellulose, the mordant may not penetrate the scales of the wool. When treated as a protein, the mordant will not be as effective on the cellulose. Distinctive dye effects can result depending on the mordant process chosen. Because silk has no scales, it can be effectively mordanted as a protein or as cellulose.

REUSE AND DISPOSAL OF TANNIN AND MORDANT BATHS

Once a solution of tannin or mordant has been used, the dyer may assume that approximately one-half of the tannin or mordant in the bath has been transferred to the fiber. The balance remains in the solution. Many dyers have learned this by experience, but it can be accurately determined by measuring the density of the liquid by using a hydrometer (see the appendix).

The reuse of a mordant bath is economical. An equal amount of fiber can be treated with tannin or mordant in the same pot by adding approximately half of the previously measured materials and more water, as needed. The solution will likely need to be reheated in order to regain optimum temperature. Production dyers will find this a useful practice.

EXAMPLE: Mordant 100 g of wool at 15 percent alum (15 g). Once the mordanting is complete, there will be approximately 7.5 g of alum in the bath. The dyer can mordant half the original amount of wool in the same bath with no additions, OR, add 7.5 g of alum and water to volume in order to mordant another 100 g of wool. This is sometimes referred to as "recharging" the pot.

Recharge of both the tannin bath and the aluminum acetate mordant on cotton, once a week, over 5 weeks, and dyed with pomegranate. 1. Original tannin and mordant; 5. 4th recharge of tannin and mordant. The amount of mordant attached to the textile increased slightly over the weeks, indicating that just less than 50% of the mordant was used each time.

Immersion Dyeing

If alum mordant baths for wool or silk are used frequently, consider keeping a pot solely for mordant application. The alum solution is acidic, will not deteriorate, and can be kept almost indefinitely. Add more water and mordant as needed. A hydrometer will help determine exactly how much alum is required to restore the solution.

Both aluminum acetate and alum/soda ash baths can be recharged multiple times. Although both these mordants will become cloudy over time, it does not diminish their effectiveness. Tannin baths can be recharged several times until a mold begins to form. Once mold develops, discard the tannin bath.

When a tannin or mordant bath must be disposed of, either solution will be mildly acetic. They may be poured onto acid-loving plants (e.g., rhododendron, azalea, camellia, or holly) in your personal garden. If the studio uses a septic system, neutralize the solutions with a small amount of soda ash before pouring them down the drain. If the studio waste disposal is part of a city water treatment, it may be poured down the drain without concern.

Consider using a leftover alum solution combined with a dye bath when making a lake pigment.

Refer to recipe 16.

Dyeing

Dyeing is the process by which the water-soluble dye attaches to the mordant or the fiber. The textile should be completely wetted out to ensure the most even penetration of dye. The amount of liquid in a dye bath is not critical but should provide sufficient volume to immerse the textile and ensure uniform dyeing. The textile must be evenly exposed to the dye in solution, with room to move around. It is more difficult to attain an even dyeing on fabric than on yarn because of the tendency of fabric to float and fold. For this reason, fabric requires more liquid in the dye pot than do yarns of equal weight.

Extract the dye from source material (plant or insect). Refer to chapter 3 for suggested dye quantities and extraction methods. Strain any solid material prior to dyeing. OR, dissolve a dye extract in water before adding to the dye bath. Some extracts are more difficult to dissolve and may require longer soaking times to ensure that there are no solid particles. Add the dye to the dye pot along with a suitable amount of water.

Any dyeing instructions that are specific to a dye (e.g., temperature, pH, or time in the dye bath) can be found in chapter 3, listed under the individual dye. These specific dye recommendations apply to the use of extracts as well as extractions from dye source material.

Dyeing Mordanted Textiles

Place the pre-mordanted, wetted-out textile into a bath with plenty of water and the extracted dye. Dye baths should begin at a low temperature (approximately 38–48°C/100–120°F). Slowly increase the temperature over 45 minutes to 1 hour to reach an ideal dyeing temperature:

- ≈70°C/160°F for silk, ≈80°C/180°F for wool (or just below a simmer)

Cellulose fibers may be brought to a boil, unless the high temperature will damage the dye. Refer to dye information specific to the dye being used. Some dyes, such as madder, perform best at lower temperatures. Maintain the dye bath temperature for 30 to 60 minutes or until the desired color has been reached. The dye will continue to penetrate the textile over the duration of the dye bath, binding to the mordant and forming an insoluble lake inside the textile.

Some dyes will attach to the textile very quickly while others attach more slowly. If a dye contains both flavonoid dye and tannin (e.g., henna, rhubarb, pomegranate), the flavonoids will attach to the mordant and fiber first. As the textile remains in the bath, the tannin will attach to the textile and oxidize, and the color will deepen and darken.

Gently move the textile in the dye bath frequently. This ensures even dyeing and avoids hot spots at the bottom of the dye pot. Some dyers keep the textile moving constantly. A stainless steel shelf or rack placed at the bottom of the dye pot will separate the textile from the bottom surface, where hot spots can occur. If the volume of the dye bath decreases during dyeing, additional hot water should be added to bring the level of the liquid back to the original volume.

If the desired color is reached within the first 15 minutes of the dye process, move the textile to a "stop bath," which is a plain water bath of a similar

| 15 MINUTES | 30 MINUTES | 45 MINUTES | 1 HOUR |

OPPOSITE: Effect of time in heated dye bath: alum-mordanted wool, dyed with madder root (top) and henna (bottom), 15 minutes to 1 hour in the dye bath. Heat and time result in deeper colors and more penetration of the dye. Yellow flavonoids in the henna attach first, while the darker tannins attach more slowly.

Chapter 5

Immersion Dyeing

temperature. Complete the hourlong heated process in the "dye-free" stop bath. This will ensure that the dye penetrates into the textile.

After dyeing, allow the textile to cool to room temperature in the bath. The textile will continue to absorb dye as it cools. The color on the textile will always appear darker when wet and will lighten as it dries.

Rinse the cooled textile and apply a post-mordant immediately, if it is to be used. Finish the textile with a thorough cleaning.

POST-MORDANTING AND PH MODIFIERS

Iron is the most common mordant used for post-mordanting. It may be applied to mordant dyes or to those applied without mordants. The iron may be in the form of ferrous sulfate or ferrous acetate. Both of these will darken or "sadden" the hue and will increase the lightfastness of the dye. Ferrous acetate is recommended because it is less damaging to all fibers.

Apply iron to the textile by using a separate bath after the initial dyeing is completed, rather than adding iron directly to the dye bath. The advantage of a separate post-mordant bath is that the dye bath will be preserved for use as an exhaust dye bath or for making a lake. It is also easier to control the amount of iron that attaches to the textile.

When a dyed textile is immersed in a post-mordant iron bath, the mordant will permanently bind with the dye in the textile, further fixing the dye and modifying the color. The use of an iron pot during dyeing will also shift the color. The use of a copper or brass pot during dyeing, or afterward, will shift the color slightly toward green and improve lightfastness.

Always be very careful with iron in any form. It can easily contaminate surfaces, dye pots, and any other tools with which it comes into contact. Once iron attaches to a dyed textile, its effect is not reversible.

Some dye colors, cochineal in particular, can be dramatically altered by pH changes. These adjustments are usually made with the additional of an acid. The acid can be added directly to the dye bath or by using a post-dye treatment. When the acid is added directly to the dye bath, the colors are more stable.

Refer to recipe 13, 14 and 15.

FINISHING

After the textile has been removed from the dye bath and any post-mordant bath, it must be rinsed and cleaned thoroughly.

Refer to chapter 9,
"Finishing of Dyed and Printed Textiles."

RECOMMENDATIONS FOR MORDANT AND DYE BATHS

	MORDANTING		
	Wool	**Silk**	**Cellulose**
Heat	Usually	No	No
Tannin prior to mordanting	No	No	Yes, unless applying a concentrated mordant and dunging
Cream of tartar	Yes but only if needed	No	No

ADDITIONS TO DYE BATH			
	Wool	Silk	Cellulose
Vinegar	Yes, limited effect	Yes, limited effect	No
Cream of tartar	Yes	Yes	No
Citric acid	Yes	No	No
Tin and Cream of tartar	Yes	Yes	No

POST-DYE MORDANTS			
	Wool	Silk	Cellulose
Ferrous sulfate	Yes	No	No
Ferrous acetate	Yes	Yes	Yes

Leftover Dye Baths and Lake Pigments

When dyeing is complete and dye remains in the bath, it can be used immediately for "exhaust dyeing." Dye baths cannot be stored for any length of time. They will soon develop mold, and the dye will deteriorate.

An alternative is to bind the soluble dye to aluminum, turning it into a concentrated lake pigment. The addition of alum and soda ash will precipitate the pigment so that it can be separated from the water and strained. The result is a paste-like pigment. The addition of an essential oil (e.g., clove oil) prevents bacterial growth, and the lake pigment can be stored indefinitely. The lake pigment can be used for split-lake dyeing or direct application of pigments. Alternatively, the pigment can be dried and ground for use in watercolors or other dry-pigment applications.

🌿 Refer to recipe 16.

A lake pigment made from a cochineal dye bath. Most of the dye in the solution has been bound to the alum mordant, and the lake has precipitated. The clear liquid on top is ready to be poured off before the lake is strained.

Chapter 5
Immersion Dyeing

Dyeing with Dyes That Do Not Require Mordants

Some dyes (e.g., black walnut hulls, cutch, and henna) form bonds with a protein textile without the presence of a mordant. The dye process is the same as that required for a mordant dye, the only difference being that the textile is not mordanted. These dyes typically require long, slow dye baths, allowing plenty of time for the dye to penetrate and bind directly to the fiber. They require a long time to reach maximum depth of color,

and it is not unusual to sustain such a dye bath up to 4 hours. Cool the textile in the bath overnight to produce the deepest colors.

The bonds made with these dyes are not as resistant to washing as those made with mordants. Dyes applied directly without a mordant should not be overdyed, since some of the dye will be released from the textile in a heated immersion bath.

Dye made from fresh black walnut hulls, used directly on wool with no mordant. Time in dye bath: 1 hour, 2 hours, 4 hours, and overnight to achieve the deepest color.

Alternative Immersion Dye Processes

ONE-BATH ACID DYE

When select dyes are combined with tannin and an acid, they will readily attach to a protein fiber without a mordant, behaving like an acid dye. This is an older process that was reintroduced to dyers by dyer and researcher Michel Garcia. In some parts of the world, alum was rare, expensive, and difficult to obtain. Dyers devised a one-bath method of dyeing in which all ingredients are

put into the bath together, saving both time and energy. The dye colors that result from this process are slightly different from those obtained when using a mordant. This is due to the absence of a mordant, the presence of an acid, and the inclusion of tannin.

One-bath acid dyeing is suitable only for anthra–quinoid and naphthoquinoid dyes and some tannins. Flavonoids are not suitable because they always require a mordant in order to dye textiles.

ALUMINUM   ONE-BATH ACID DYE
MORDANT

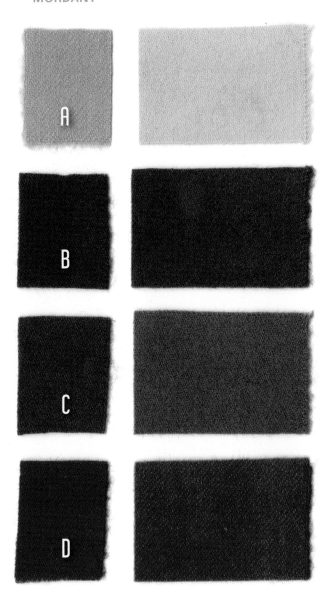

Tannin readily attaches to the dye and helps the dye bind to the textile. Gallic tannins are preferred because of the high tannin content, and their impact on dye color is minimal. The tannin contributes to the excellent lightfastness.

The acid keeps the dye dissolved and enhances the electrical attraction between dye and fiber. Acetic acid (white vinegar) or citric acid can be used. Acetic acid can evaporate during the dyeing, so it is important to monitor and maintain the pH of the dye bath.

🌿 Refer to recipe 17.

Since no mordant bath is required, this process can save time as a method of dyeing in a single dye bath. When dyeing a textile constructed of both protein and cellulose fibers, the dye will attach only to the protein, making it suitable for cross-dye techniques. Cellulose has no electrical charge, and it will not dye with an acid dye.

These acid dyes are extremely lightfast, but they do not have the same washfastness qualities as dyes that use a mordant. They will withstand normal cleaning but should not be heated or overdyed, since the dye will release in the heated bath.

🌿 Refer to chapter 9, "Finishing of Dyed and Printed Textiles."

Comparison of the same dyes applied on aluminum-mordanted wool and as one-bath acid dyes: A. rhubarb, B. lac, C. cochineal, D. madder.

Immersion Dyeing

DYES SUITABLE FOR ONE-BATH ACID DYE APPLICATION

Common Name	Latin Name	Chemical Group	Color
Cochineal	Dactyopius coccus	Anthraquinoid	Red
Docks and Sorrel	Rumex spp	Anthraquinoid	Gold to Brown
Henna	Lawsonia intermis	Naphthoquinoid	Gold/Orange/Brown
Madder, European and Indian	Rubia tinctorium and R. cordifolia	Anthraquinoid	Orange
Lac	Kerria lacca	Anthraquinoid	Red
Pomegranate	Punica granatum	Tannin	Gold
Rhubarb Rheum spp	Rheum spp	Anthraquinoid	Yellow/gold
Black Walnut	Juglans nigra	Naphthaquinoid	Brown

Cross-dye effect on fabric constructed of wool and cotton: A. fabric dyed with indigo only, B. fabric dyed with rhubarb root, using one-bath acid dye application, C. fabric dyed with indigo, followed by rhubarb.

Cross-dyeing by using a resist applied to fabric constructed of wool and cotton, first dyed with indigo by using a resist, followed by one-bath acid dyes (rhubarb and cochineal).

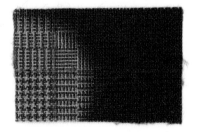

DYEING WITH A SPLIT LAKE-PIGMENT

A dye that has been converted into a lake pigment and stored (recipe 16) can be made soluble once again and used for dyeing protein. Citric acid is strong enough to split/break the bond between the dye and the mordant that originally made the lake. Once that bond is broken, both the dye and mordant become soluble once again and are able to enter the textile and partly re-form there.

When a protein textile is immersed in the bath, the mordant and dye will both attach to the fibers and the lake will re-form in the textile, to some degree, during rinsing and neutralizing. Post-mordanting will further ensure the forming of the lake.

This is a recycling process. Since the dye lake was originally made from a used dye bath, it difficult to determine the exact amount or quality of dye present in the lake, and dye colors may not always be predictable.

🌿 Refer to recipe 18.

Immersion dyeing on wool, using a split lake-pigment: A. madder, B. lac, C. cutch, D. pomegranate, E. weld, F. madder/lac combination, G. cochineal.

SLOW DYEING WITHOUT HEAT

Extended time in a dye bath can substitute for a heated dye bath. Begin the dye process with warm or hot tap water, if possible. Otherwise, dyeing time will be longer or less of the dye will attach.

If using dye source material, first make a heated decoction of the dye and strain before adding the mordanted textile. Slow dyeing can also be done with dye extracts or by using finely ground plant material added directly to the bath. Add enough water to immerse the textile. Stir the dye bath occasionally. Maximum color is usually reached within 4 to 5 days, depending on the dye and the fiber. After a few days, the plant material may begin to mold and some dyes will deteriorate. Certain dyes (e.g., cutch) never reach their full depth of color without heat.

Although results may not be identical to a heated process, this is a viable alternative if heat is not available or if using a heat-sensitive wax resist for batik.

Immersion Dyeing

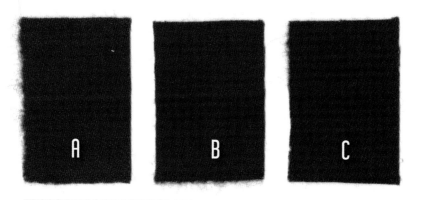

Slow dyeing on wool. Madder dye bath was made with hot tap water and no additional heat: A. 24 hours in dye bath, B. 7 days in dye bath, C. traditional heated dye bath.

Slow dyeing on silk, madder, cutch, and weld. Top row: heated dye bath, bottom row: 24 hours in dye bath with no heat. Weld and madder dyed the silk strongly after only 24 hours, but the cutch never achieved full color without heat.

CHAPTER 6
Indigo

This chapter explains how the indigo is reduced in the vat, how to make an organic indigo vat, how to dye in the vat, and—very important—how to maintain the vats. Specific dye amounts and recipes are in chapter 11.

Indigo Reduction

After the indigo pigment has been extracted from the plant, it is not water soluble. The indigo must be converted into a soluble form, called "leuco indigo" or "indigo white," which is actually pale yellow in color. This comes from the Greek word *leukos*, which means "white" or "lacking color." Once the indigo is soluble it can be used to dye the textile. The conversion to soluble indigo is accomplished by using one of these methods:

- Slow fermentation by using organic materials. This process takes many days and is often very pungent.

- "Quick" alkaline reduction with sugars or plants that contain sugars or pectins. These vats convert to fermentation over time.

- Mineral reduction by using iron or zinc. These vats require a higher pH than the other vats and are only suitable for use with cellulose fibers. Protein fibers will be damaged by the high alkalinity. Mineral reduction was used for traditional resist dyeing from the sixteenth century onward, and in the production of textile "blue prints" all over Europe.

- Reduction chemicals such as thiourea dioxide or sodium hydrosulfite. Though quick and effective, these chemical reduction agents emit an unpleasant odor and pose health and environmental issues. The chemicals are sulfur based, and the odor results from sulfur compounds such as sulfur dioxide, which can be harmful to breathe. This vat is the most common method used in production dyeing but should only be done in a well-ventilated area and with care.

Michel Garcia introduced the "quick sugar / plant reduction" and "mineral/iron reduction" vats to contemporary dyers around the world. Although they are based on historical dye practices, many dyers had not experienced these vats until he reintroduced them. Since the vats are safe and easy to use and produce excellent results, we have chosen to focus our attention on these.

The indigo vats use either plant sugars or iron to rapidly start the reduction, which begins in just a few minutes. The vats are usually ready for use after 12–48 hours. These vats are relatively easy to maintain, do not have unpleasant odors, and can be made successfully in almost any size. With proper care, the vats can be maintained for long periods of time.

All indigo vats require a high alkalinity (high pH) for proper functioning. The plants, carbohydrates, sugars, or iron used for the indigo vat are reductive, which means that they oxidize and give off electrons. In the environment of the alkaline vat, reduction is even stronger. The indigo molecule is forced to receive the two negatively charged electrons, which is a reduction; this influences the oxygen bonds of the indigo pigment, making the indigo molecule attractive to the positively charged part of the water molecule. In this way the

indigo becomes soluble. Reduction is often described as "removing oxygen."

Once it is soluble, the dye is able to penetrate the textile. When the textile is removed from the alkaline vat and exposed to oxygen, the process reverses itself, and the indigo becomes insoluble blue again but is now in the textile.

The "quick" sugar / plant vats gradually transform to fermentation vats over the first 2–3 weeks. Sugars continue to oxidize into different organic acids, which slowly lower the pH of the vat. The sugars must be replaced, and this is what it means to "feed the vat." The success of the vat relies on active reduction and a high pH, which is maintained by the addition of lime as needed. All these elements must be kept in balance.

The mineral vat uses ferrous sulfate to reduce the vat. The iron is a reduction agent. The iron is converted to iron oxide, but it does not oxidize into acids. As a result the pH remains high. The iron does not dull or darken the color of the indigo as it would with other dyes.

insoluble indigo   reduction   soluble leuco indigo

oxidation

Chemical formula for reduction and oxidation of indigo. The double oxygen bonds of the indigo pigment are changed into single bonds during reduction, making it possible for the indigo molecule to dissolve in the vat. The process reverses after the textile is dyed: indigo oxidizes and becomes insoluble once again.

Preparing the Organic Reduction Vats

Refer to recipes 19–22 for specific quantities and instructions to make each of the vats

In addition to water, the indigo vat is composed of three ingredients:

- indigo
- alkali
- reduction material (sugar, fruit, plant, or iron)

THE SIZE OF THE VAT

An indigo vat needs to be of sufficient volume to allow the textile to be completely immersed. Small-scale indigo dyeing is typically done one textile at a time. The vessel and dye must accommodate the textile with sufficient room for the textile to move in the vat for even dye "exposure." Textiles must not be allowed to come in contact with the bottom of the vat, where unreduced materials settle. The ideal vessel for an indigo vat is tall and narrow and made of either stainless steel or plastic. This shape also minimizes exposure to oxygen on the surface of the vat. Aluminum is not suitable because the high alkalinity of the vat will corrode the aluminum.

A 1 L vat may be large enough to dye small samples. Textiles that are compressed by using *shibori* resists can be dyed in a relatively small vat. Greater capacity will be required to dye larger textiles. A 5-gallon (≈19 L) polypropylene pail is a good size and shape for most small studio dyeing projects. When production dyeing is a concern, consider using several small vats instead of a single large one. This allows for indigo vats of different strengths, and as one vat is being used for dyeing, another can be resting.

WATER AND TEMPERATURE

It is best to start all of the organic vats by using hot water (approximately 90°C/190°F). Hot water contains less oxygen than cold water, and the heat helps the reduction to proceed more quickly. Once the vat is made, it will cool to the ambient room temperature. Vats will begin reduction more quickly in warm weather, but they can be maintained at a wide range of room temperatures. (16°C/60°F to 32°C/90°F). If begun with cool water, reduction will be much slower.

HOW MUCH INDIGO?

Indigo is a highly concentrated pigment, and only a small quantity is needed to make a successful dye vat. The amount of indigo in the vat might range from 1 to 10 g/L of liquid volume. All other ingredients are calculated based on the amount of indigo. One or two grams of indigo per liter are enough if the vat is for a one-time use only, or if producing light colors. When a vat is to be used heavily or maintained for a long time, or if deep colors are desired, start the vat by using 8–10 g of indigo per liter. Darkest indigo colors are achieved by using multiple dips in the vat. Additional indigo may be added at any time during the life of the vat.

PREPARATION OF THE INDIGO PIGMENT

Measure the desired amount of indigo and place it into a strong plastic jar with a tight-fitting lid along with a few marbles or clean, smooth pebbles. Pour in sufficient warm water to cover the pigment, close the jar tightly, and shake it vigorously for a few minutes. This will crush the indigo pigment into the finest possible particles, while also hydrating it. This ensures that the reduction can access each molecule of dye easily once it is added to the vat.

ALKALI

Slaked lime (calcium hydroxide) [Ca(OH)2] is used to achieve and maintain the alkalinity of the vats. This is a strong alkaline, sometimes referred to as "pickling lime," and is easy to obtain. Since it is a lightweight powder, and easily airborne, a dust mask or respirator is recommended while measuring the dry powder.

Traditionally, indigo vats were made with wood ash lye. Most of the chemical vats specify sodium hydroxide, which is commercially produced lye.

Calcium oxide, or quicklime [CaO], may be used, but we recommend it only with reservations because it is very unstable and must be hydrated first.

 CAUTION: The hydration of calcium oxide develops a great deal of heat and should be done very carefully, in a glass container with physical protection and in a controlled environment. It is safest to use the already hydrated product [Ca(OH)$_2$].

Chapter 6
Indigo

THE REDUCTION MATERIAL

Effective sugar/plant-based reduction materials include:

- Natural sugars from fruits and vegetables: apple, banana, grape, mango, pear, turnip, zucchini. Also, fructose, barley sugar, glucose, honey, fructose, maltose, and glucose. Cane sugar and sugar refined from beets (table sugars) are not reductive and will not reduce an indigo vat.

- Pectins, which are compound sugars. They can be extracted from citrus fruit rinds by boiling and are also found in some fruits and vegetables.

- Organic matter such as madder root, rhubarb root, or henna leaves, all of which contain dye and compound sugars. The dyes may be extracted from these materials before they are used for indigo reduction. Henna also contains a precursor that oxidizes into the dye lawsone, and this oxidation will help reduce the indigo.

Mineral reduction material:

- Ferrous sulfate is reductive in alkaline conditions. It oxidizes into ferric sulfate and simultaneously reduces the indigo into the soluble leuco indigo.

Small indigo vats made by using varying amounts of indigo: 2 g, 5 g, and 8 g per L. The color of the leuco indigo is lighter in the weaker vats, as is the dye color, since there is less indigo available for reduction. The amount of unreduced material on the bottom of the vat also increases with the amount of indigo in the vat.

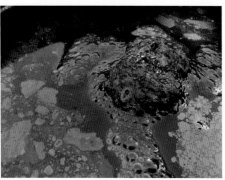

The surface of a healthy indigo vat, showing large bubbles and a metallic sheen on the surface.

After the Vat Is Made

As soon as the vat is made (according to recipes 19, 20, 21, or 22), stir the dye vat with a strong centrifugal motion, creating a vortex, to be sure that all ingredients are incorporated. When the vat is stirred in this manner, a minimal amount of oxygen is introduced. Wait about 30 minutes and stir again. The first bubbles should appear on the surface. Cover the vat loosely to prevent introduction of oxygen.

Stir and rest the vat a couple more times during the first 24 hours while the reduction is taking place.

The vat is ready for use when there is a coppery film and dark-blue bubbles on the surface. This may take from a few hours to 2 days, depending on the ambient temperature and the reduction material that was used. The liquid below the surface will turn green and will eventually turn yellow or bronze in color. This is the leuco color and indicates reduction has been achieved. The liquid should be free of floating particles. Solid particles that are not reduced (excess indigo, lime, reduction material) will precipitate to the bottom of the vessel.

If dyeing is attempted before the indigo is completely reduced, the color will not be lightfast or washfast. During the first week, additional indigo in the vat will continue to be reduced.

DYEING WITH INDIGO

The vat will form both a metallic "skin" of unreduced indigo on the surface of the vat, and larger bubbles, known as a "flower." This can be moved aside or removed before dyeing. If not removed, the unreduced indigo will temporarily attach to the textile but will easily rinse off.

The textile should be scoured, if necessary, and completely wetted out before dyeing in the vat (with the exception of dyeing by using indigo paste resist). Squeeze any excess water from the textile before dyeing. Wearing gloves, carefully lower the textile into the vat and ensure that it is completely immersed. Gently move the textile in the vat, making sure that all parts of the textile can be reached by the indigo. Indigo does not penetrate as easily as other dyes and will dye only the fiber with which it comes into contact. A fold in the textile or a tightly tied skein will act as a resist. This characteristic of indigo makes it an ideal dye for resist techniques, such as *shibori*, but to achieve even dyeing, the textile must be moved gently and frequently. If the vat is large enough, the textile can be lowered into the vat in such a way that it is exposed on all surfaces, and no movement is necessary.

An open basket or net can be used to contain the textile. When lowered into the vat, it will prevent contact with the solid particles at the bottom of the vat. The textile will not dye properly if it comes into contact with this material.

All activity in the indigo vat should be gentle and calm, disturbing the surface as little as possible. Slow, careful movement avoids the introduction of oxygen to the vat, which will cause the vat to go out of reduction quickly.

Each immersion into the vat should be at least 10–20 minutes in duration to allow for optimum dye penetration. A lengthy dip is required to allow the dye into the fiber. A short dip of 1 to 2 minutes will result in dyeing only the surface and will not be lightfast or washfast, and the dye will more easily rub off the textile. The deepest indigo blues are achieved by long, repeated dips in the vat. Multiple dips will help even out the dye, which might be irregular after a single dip.

When pale blue colors are desired, dye with a weak indigo vat, rather than a short immersion time in a strong vat.

Once the immersion in the vat is complete, squeeze the dye from the textile below the surface of the vat, so that minimal oxygen will be introduced and most of the

dye remains in the vat. Rinse the textile immediately in a vessel filled with cool tap water. This initial rinse will remove any unattached indigo and begin the oxidation process. Hang the textile on a line until it is completely oxidized. The color will change from yellow to green and finally to blue. The indigo is bound to the textile only by affinity until it has been oxidized, when it becomes insoluble inside the fiber. The textile may be redipped in the vat for deeper colors only after it is fully oxidized. Allow at least 30–40 minutes for complete oxidation. Folds or tight ties on the textile can prevent full oxidation. Allow the textile to dry slowly in a shaded place to complete the dye process before neutralizing or finishing.

Although indigo is used to dye all types of natural fibers, it has the greatest affinity for cellulose. Cellulose takes up the indigo dye more readily than a protein fiber and will produce a deeper blue color. Additionally, the high pH of the vat can be damaging to protein fibers.

Vats that are made by using sugar, plants, or fruit will have a pH of approximately 12.0 at the start of use. The pH must be this high to allow the indigo vat to go into reduction but is not required for maintaining reduction or dyeing. Once the reduction is well underway, the reduction materials will create different organic acids, while slowly lowering the pH level to approximately 10.0.

The pH of the mineral vat will remain close to 12.0 and should never be used to dye protein.

Protein fibers can be dyed with indigo, but caution must be used because of the alkalinity. A pH of 12.0 is suitable for dyeing cellulose fibers, but protein fibers will be damaged. Wool or silk should be dyed only after the pH has fallen to 9.5 or 10.0. If wool is dyed in a vat that is too alkaline, it will emit a sulfur smell when it is neutralized. This is a clear indication that the pH of the vat was too high for the textile and that some fiber damage has occurred.

LOWERING THE PH FOR PROTEIN DYEING

Once the pH of the sugar, fruit, or plant vat has begun to fall, the pH can be further lowered for safer dyeing of protein fibers with the addition of hide glue or gelatin. Weigh the glue or gelatin at 1 percent w.o.f. and dissolve it in a little hot water for several hours before use. Add the dissolved glue or gelatin to the vat just before dyeing. These are protein substances and will absorb excess alkalinity before precipitating to the bottom of the vat. The indigo vat can continue to be used for dyeing cellulose.

Indigo on various fibers: A. cotton, B. linen, C. silk shantung, D. tussah silk, E. wool. All dyed for the same amount of time, using the same vat.

Pale colors with indigo: A. 1-minute immersion in strong vat, B. 20-minute immersion in a weak indigo vat. Short immersion time in the strong vat results in uneven dye that sits only on the surface of the textile. A long immersion results in a dye that penetrates the fiber.

NEUTRALIZING THE TEXTILE

Once all dyeing and oxidation are complete, the textile must be neutralized. Lime that remains in the textile will be damaging to both the textile and the dye. Make a weak acid bath of white vinegar (5% acetic acid). Add approximately 15 ml of vinegar to 1 L of cold water. Mix enough solution to completely immerse the textile. Allow the textile to remain in this neutralizing bath for at least 15 minutes; heavy or dense textiles will require a longer time. Vinegar will neutralize any lime left in the textile, the color will brighten, and the indigo dye will stabilize. Remove the textile from the vinegar bath and rinse.

FINISHING

Finish the textile with a thorough, heated cleaning as described in chapter 9.

Building deep blue colors with indigo on cotton. The lightest blue is a result of a single immersion in the vat, while the deepest blue was dyed six times, oxidizing completely between each immersion in the vat.

Indigo

MAINTENANCE OF THE SUGAR, FRUIT, AND PLANT VATS

Maintaining an indigo vat is very much like caring for a pet. One must stir the vat, feed the vat, watch the pH, observe the surface, and sometimes make a good guess about what it needs.

Each of the vats contains unreduced indigo, excess organic reduction material, and lime, all of which settles to the bottom of the vat. Dyeing occurs in the clear leuco liquid above the sediment. As the vat is used, some of the sediment may be disturbed and the vat will get cloudy or the color will change to green, indicating that there is unreduced indigo floating in the vat. When this happens, it is time to feed, stir, and rest the vat.

Feeding or Replenishing the Vat

Add a small amount of additional reduction material after each use. The reduction material is consumed as it reduces the indigo. Use any of the recommended reduction materials (e.g., fructose, liquid extracted from cooked fruit or plant material) to boost the reduction. A 5-gallon vat will easily absorb about 3 tablespoons of fructose powder during a dyeing session. If the vat is used heavily, it might require additional replenishment.

Stirring

After the dye session is complete, the sediment must be stirred up into the vat to reactivate it and keep the vat lively and healthy. Carefully loosen the material at the bottom of the vat, using a round stirring rod. Then lift the rod just above the bottom and stir, creating a strong vortex in the vat. Stop stirring or slowly move the stir rod in the opposite direction and the vortex will settle, causing bubbles to form in the center of the surface.

Allow the vat to rest until the unreduced material settles. The liquid in the vat must return to a clear leuco color before dyeing again. This may take several hours. Always keep the vat covered when it is not being used, to prevent the introduction of oxygen.

Check the pH

The pH of the vat must be above 9.0 in order to remain in reduction. Additional lime should be added occasionally, but it is not needed after every use. As the vat is used and reduction material is added, the pH of the vat will very gradually decrease. If the vat is left unused for a period of time, a week or more, the pH will also fall. To use the vat, add enough lime to increase the pH to at least 10.0 or 11.0. Because the dark-blue color of the dye will color the pH paper, it is somewhat difficult to monitor the pH with single-color pH strips. A test strip with multiple color pads or a pH meter is more accurate.

Adding More Indigo

A vat will eventually become weaker as the indigo is consumed. More dye can be added by using either of the following approaches:

- Add hydrated indigo, new reduction material, and lime in the original proportions, with enough water to dissolve these ingredients. For quickest reduction, combine these ingredients in a separate vessel to make a small concentrated vat. Once it is reduced, add the new concentrated vat to the original one.

- Make and maintain a strong "mother vat," which is a more concentrated version of the original vat. Add a portion of this mother vat to your working vat occasionally in order to boost the indigo content of the dye vat.

Instead of adding more indigo, consider maintaining the weak vat for dyeing light colors and make a new vat for full-strength dyeing.

MAINTENANCE OF THE MINERAL/IRON VAT

The iron vat does not need to be fed with additional reduction material after each use and rarely requires additional lime. The vat only needs to be stirred and rested. If additional indigo is required, make and maintain a small, concentrated "mother vat." Add some of the reduced indigo from the mother vat to boost the larger ferrous vat.

The high proportion of lime in this vat results in a larger amount of sediment than in the sugar and plant vats. Over time, the sediment will increase, leaving a smaller available space for dyeing. When the indigo is used up and the sediment is deep, it is best to discard the vat and make a new one.

TROUBLESHOOTING THE INDIGO VATS

When the indigo vat is producing beautiful blue colors, this is an indication that everything is in balance. On the other hand, when the color seems weak or just doesn't seem right, something is likely out of adjustment. The problem is often with the reduction or with the pH. It will take practice to test and adjust these elements.

1. Each day the vat is used, dye a small cotton test sample, using only a single dip. Keep this in a daily log. These samples are invaluable for determining the condition of the vat.

2. The mound of bubbles at the center of the vat, often referred to as "the flower," can be used to diagnose the vat. Ideally, the vat will have a mound of large dark-blue bubbles. If the bubbles become small, it is likely that the reduction needs strengthening. If bubbles are light blue or white, the pH may be low.

3. Test the pH regularly by using pH papers or a pH meter. You can also double-check the pH results by sprinkling a small spoonful of lime on the surface of the vat. If the lime floats, then likely the pH is fine. However, if the lime is quickly absorbed down into the vat, then the pH is probably low and the vat requires additional lime.

4. When the sugar or plant vat is left idle for a week or more, the pH will decrease and additional lime is usually required. Add more reduction material as well.

5. If the color becomes weak, check the pH first. Then add reduction material. Watch the vat carefully for a few days and continue to test the color. Try adding more reduction material. If the color remains weak, the indigo may be depleted.

6. If there is plenty of indigo in the vat, and the pH is fine, yet the vat is still not dyeing well, it may need a significant boost of reduction material. Heat or cook the reduction material before adding it to the vat. The addition of warm material will speed up the reduction process.

7. Record the original amount of indigo in the vat and monitor the amount of dyeing. This will help predict the amount of dying that can be done in a vat.

8. If there is no coppery sheen or bubbles on the surface, this is usually an indication of a reduction problem. The vat needs to be fed with sugar, plants, or fruit.

9. If a dye vat forms mold on the surface, it's an indication that the pH has fallen. Mold will not form on a vat with a high pH. Remove the mold, add lime, and stir.

10. As the vat is used, the volume will slowly decrease. In order to maintain the original volume, occasionally add more liquid. Add hot water, the heated juice of fruits or plants, or some of the water used for rinsing textiles immediately after dyeing. The rinse water contains all the original ingredients of the vat.

11. When the ambient temperature is low (below 10°C/50°F), the vat may struggle to maintain reduction. Heating the vat can help with the reduction. If the vat is in a stainless steel vessel, it can be heated gently on a burner, but be careful that it doesn't go above 60°C/140°F. A plastic vessel can be placed in a hot water bath to warm it. An aquarium heater can be immersed in the vat to maintain the temperature in cold, unheated environments.

CHAPTER 7
Mixing and Shading Colors

This chapter suggests methods for controlling the depth of color, and practical methods for mixing natural dye colors.

Controlling the Amount of Dye

Natural dyers often use dyes at their full strength to achieve a strong color. If lighter values are needed, there are several approaches that can be used:

- Exhaust baths are dye baths that have already been used for dyeing and have some dye remaining. When a textile is dyed in a partly exhausted bath, lighter colors will result, but this approach doesn't always result in a predictable hue. Each natural dye source is composed of several different dyes. As the dye bath is used, the dyes deplete at different rates. A partially exhaus-

ted bath may give a slightly different hue from the original dye bath.

- Smaller amounts of dye will result in lighter values. Measurable dilute solutions can be made from dye extractions as a means of achieving the most precise dyeing of light and dark values.

- When printing on cellulose, the mordant strength controls the depth of the dye color. A weaker mordant will result in weaker dye color.

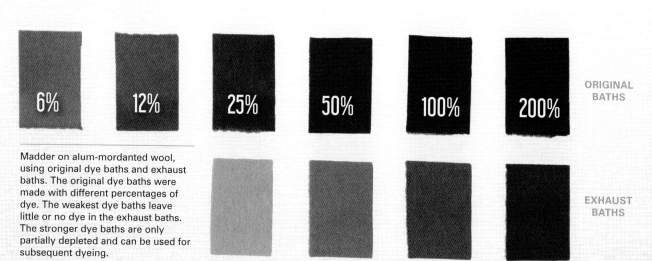

6% | 12% | 25% | 50% | 100% | 200%

ORIGINAL BATHS

EXHAUST BATHS

Madder on alum-mordanted wool, using original dye baths and exhaust baths. The original dye baths were made with different percentages of dye. The weakest dye baths leave little or no dye in the exhaust baths. The stronger dye baths are only partially depleted and can be used for subsequent dyeing.

Mixing Colors by Combining Natural Dyes

Each natural dye source produces a complex color with an undertone of other hues. This is one of the reasons for the harmonious and pleasing colors that result from natural dyes. To further enrich and expand the palette, dyes can be combined. There are two different approaches to color mixing:

- Overdye a previously dyed textile by using a secondary dye. Use a fresh dye bath or a partly exhausted one. Although it is an economical use of leftover dyes, partially exhausted baths are not always predictable or measurable. Overdyeing is NOT suitable for dyes that have been applied directly without mordants or one-bath acid dyes. These dyes are not as washfast as mordant dyes and will be released from the textile in subsequent heated baths.

- Combine two or more dyes in the same dye bath. This requires an understanding of how the colors mix. A full-strength yellow flavonoid can be dramatically changed when combined with a small amount of a stronger dye. This is an efficient approach and is also less damaging to the textile since it requires the use of only one heated bath. This is the only suitable approach for directly applied dyes and one-bath acid dyes.

When two or more colors are mixed, they should, ideally, have similar lightfastness. As the color fades, it will maintain its original tone and integrity without undesirable color shifts caused by constituent colors fading at differing rates.

Color mixing on alum-mordanted ramie. The textile was dyed with weld at full strength. Increasing amounts of a partially exhausted madder dye bath were added to the weld bath to shift the hue.

Color mixing on alum-mordanted wool. Weld is dyed at full strength with increasing amounts of a strong cochineal dye bath added to weld dye bath.

Mixing and Shading Colors

Combining Indigo with Other Natural Dyes

Indigo can be combined with mordant dyes to create greens, violets, and other mixed tones. An extended range of hues will result from different values of indigo blue. A weak indigo vat is required in order to dye light blues for the most delicate mixtures.

Most dyers learn to apply mordant dyes first, followed by indigo, but this sequence is not ideal. Mordant dyes, particularly those applied to cellulose, are sensitive to the high pH of the indigo vat and can be damaged by the alkalinity of the indigo vat. If the dye-mordant connection is damaged, the dye will be released. Optimize both the indigo and the mordant

dye by dyeing cellulose fibers first with indigo. The mordant bond to protein fibers is not as sensitive, but resulting colors will be different, depending on which dye is applied first.

Once the textile has been dyed with indigo, apply the tannin (if used for cellulose), followed by the mordant and finally the mordant dye. This sequence is not as critical when using dyes without a mordant, though the final color will be influenced by the sequence of dye application. Some dye colors are altered or darkened as a result of the alkalinity of the indigo vat.

Color mixing with indigo and mordant dyes. Silk was first dyed with indigo of three different values. Then the textile was mordanted and dyed with selected dyes: madder, cochineal, weld, and pomegranate.

Dyeing indigo first has secondary advantages. Indigo-dyed textiles always have an alkaline residue that must be neutralized. Since tannins and mordants are both acidic, post-indigo treatment with tannin and mordant will further ensure a thorough neutralization of the textile. The post-indigo dye bath takes the place of boiling out the indigo in the finishing process. With practice, the dyer can learn to control the final color by the shade of indigo applied to the textile first.

COTTON

WOOL

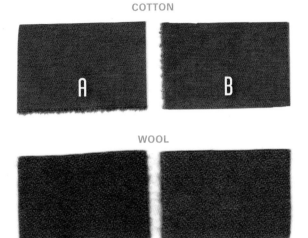

Dye sequence comparison on cotton and wool: A. weld overdyed with indigo, B. indigo, mordanted and then overdyed with weld. When indigo follows a mordant dye, the color will always be more blue than if indigo is dyed first, followed by the mordant and dye.

Pale indigo shades from a weak vat are used to achieve the most delicate greens. Three values of indigo on cotton, followed by mordant and myrobalan dye.

Black walnut and indigo dye sequence. Although no mordant was used, the alkaline vat can affect tannins and other dyes. Different colors will result, depending on which dye was used first: A. black walnut hull overdyed with indigo, B. indigo overdyed with black walnut.

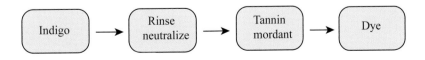

Recommended dye sequence for mixing indigo and mordant dyes on cellulose.

85

Mixing and Shading Colors

Black with Natural Dyes

Black (or near-black) shades can be achieved on a textile by using a combination of iron and tannins, but iron should only be used in very small amounts because of its damaging effect on most fibers. For this reason, we recommend that black be created by using a combination of dyes.

There are several classic approaches to creating black on a textile by using natural dyes. They all utilize a full spectrum of strong color that is layered on the textile.

• Mix three primary colors. Begin with a deep indigo blue, followed by aluminum mordant and a strong red such as madder, cochineal, or lac. Judge the color, and if the hue is too "purple," overdye with a small amount of weld or other yellow to balance the color.

• Beginning with a very deep indigo blue, mordant the textile and overdye it by using a condensed tannin (cutch or quebracho) or black walnut. All these dyes have tannins with red tones and will balance the blue of the indigo. A very small amount of iron (not more than 1–2% w.o.f.) can be added if required.

• When dyeing wool, start by using naturally colored gray or brown fibers. Follow either of the approaches listed above, but far less dye will be required in order to obtain black.

Dye sequences to achieve black with natural dye:

A. silk: 5 dips in indigo, aluminum mordant, strong cochineal dye, weld dye. B. ramie: 3 dips in indigo, cutch

applied in unheated tannin bath, 1% ferrous acetate postmordant. C. ramie: 3 dips in indigo, tannin and aluminum mordant, strong madder dye.

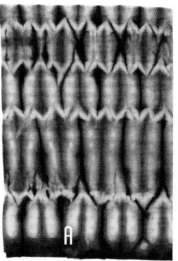

Black, using a resist: A. black was dyed on the resisted textile by dyeing first with indigo then cutch and iron, B. resist pattern was dyed in indigo, followed by mordanting of whole cloth and madder dye.

CHAPTER 8
Printing

This chapter discusses several approaches to printing by using natural dyes, including traditional mordant printing and direct printing of dye combined with a mordant. The application of natural pigments is also explained. Printing applications with indigo include indigo resist pastes, an alkaline indigo paste for direct printing, and a safe discharge solution for indigo. Specific recipes for all these applications are in chapter 11.

Printing is the general term for local, direct application of color on fabric or yarn. The application can be made by brush, sponge, stencil, screen, or printing block. The paste can be thickened to various degrees, depending on the method used and the desired effect. The general thickening agent is a natural gum.

Printing with Mordant Dyes

Successful printing requires that both mordants and dyes be bound to the textile. The mordant is required only where there is dye. Historically, the mordant was never applied to the whole textile. If the entire surface contains mordant, any excess dye released during the finishing and cleaning can bind to the mordant on the background, marring the final print.

A thickener is required in order to make print pastes from mordants or dyes. Guar gum is recommended. It is inexpensive, readily available, and holds up well in the acidic mordants. Gum tragacanth can be used, but it is often more difficult to source this gum. Sodium alginate, the substance that is most often used to thicken synthetic dyes, should not be used to thicken mordants.

When sodium alginate is combined with mordants, an insoluble, rubberlike compound will be produced. Print pastes can be applied by using a brush, printing blocks, stencils, or silkscreen.

Printing with natural dyes was traditionally done on cellulose textiles. Some techniques are suitable for silk. Printing processes are generally not considered suitable for most wool textiles, since the printed mordants and dyes do not easily penetrate beyond the scales of the wool fibers, and much of the dye remains on the surface. The final results of a printed textile will always reflect the quality and surface of the textile itself.

There are two primary approaches for printing with natural mordant dyes:

Chapter 8
Printing

Mordant printing: This is the classical approach for printing on cotton. Historically, it was called "the dyed style."

Mordants are printed directly onto the textile where the pattern is intended. The textile is then dyed in a heated immersion bath. The dye will attach permanently only where the mordants have been applied. Mordant printing results in better penetration of the cellulose fiber than direct printing of dye and mordants.

Because of protein's inherent affinity to attract dye, most dyes will make a permanent attachment to the background during the immersion-dyeing process, although there is no mordant. For this reason, mordant printing is not suitable for protein fibers.

Direct application of dye and mordant: Dye extracts can be used in combination with a mordant and an acid. The acid prevents the formation of the lake and keeps the dye and mordant soluble in the paste. The components are thickened and are applied directly onto the textile. This process is suitable for cellulose, silk, and, to a limited extent, lightweight wools.

MORDANT PRINTING: "THE DYED STYLE"

The goal of mordant printing is to fix the mordant locally on the textile. Concentrated aluminum and iron mordants are used in the form of aluminum acetate and ferrous acetate. The mordants are thickened with gum for printing but can also be used without the gum

for a less controlled "watercolor" effect. The acetate mordants can be mixed together in any proportion to achieve various shades with a single dye bath. Aluminum acetate is usually applied at full strength but may be diluted for lighter tints. Ferrous acetate is frequently applied in a dilute form to achieve lighter shades.

Tannin is not required when using concentrated mordants for printing, and in most cases is not used. When tannin combines with any amount of iron, dark or black tones will result, making it impossible to achieve the more subtle shades from the dyes. When specific effects from the tannin and iron are desired, the textile can be treated with tannin either before or after the application of mordant.

After the mordants are applied to the textile, they must air-dry completely, preferably overnight. During the drying process, both the water and the acetic acid, a constituent of the acetate, evaporate. The dried textile should no longer smell of vinegar. If any odor remains, finish the evaporation by using a dry iron (no steam) to fully evaporate the mordant. A drying box or a portable hairdryer can be used in damp climates or rainy weather to assist with the drying process.

During the drying, the mordants precipitate onto the textile in the form of metal oxides. Aluminum acetate becomes aluminum oxide. Ferrous acetate becomes iron oxide (rust), changing to a rusty brown color.

The very small amount of "rust" that ferrous acetate deposits on the textile is far less damaging than "rust printing," which deposits a large amount of iron. Ferrous acetate has relatively little iron, and that amount is carefully controlled when the mordant is mixed.

Sequence of mordant and dye application for printing in "the dyed style."

"Dunging" is required to fix the mordant onto the textile. It completes the process, ensuring that all the acid has been neutralized and the mordants are precipitated in the textile. Originally, the dunging solution was made of dried cow dung. The phosphates contained in the dung are the active ingredients. Today, dyers use chalk (calcium carbonate). Chalk acts as a mild alkali, but only when an acid is present. When wheat bran is added to the "dung" solution, its enzymes help dissolve and remove the gum from the thickened mordant. If the gum is not completely removed, it will resist the dye.

Once fixed, the mordants will not migrate to other areas of the textile. The textile may be dyed immediately in an immersion dye bath, or it can be dried and stored for future dyeing.

The dung solution can be reused multiple times. The chalk will settle to the bottom of the vessel but can be stirred back into suspension before each use. When the chalk solution becomes dark as a result of excess iron, it should be discarded and replaced with a fresh one.

If the gum in the mordant or dye paste clogs a silkscreen, the screen can be easily cleaned, using a solution made by soaking a small amount of wheat bran in warm water.

Mordants that are used in printing can be stored for only a few days. They should be kept in a cool place and carefully covered to prevent the evaporation of the acetic acid. If it is kept too long, the gum will thin out and the mordant will become inactive. For this reason, mix only small amounts that can be used quickly.

 Refer to recipe 23, 24, and 25.

Dyeing and Choosing Dyes

When calculating the amount of dye for textiles that have been mordant printed, approximate the proportion of the surface where mordant has been applied. The dye will attach only where there is a mordant. Dye the mordant-printed textile in an immersion dye bath according to instructions in chapter 5.

Some dyes are better suited for mordant printing than others. The best dyes will produce a range of color with the various mordants and a relatively dye-free background that requires minimal cleaning. Weld and other flavonoids, pomegranate, and cutch leave the background relatively clean and are excellent choices for mordant printing. Madder, a traditional dye for mordant printing, always requires vigorous boiling to clean dye from the background. Cochineal will stain very little, while some lac extracts require a long boil to remove dye from the background. Black walnut will leave a stain on the background that is impossible to remove, and, as a result, might not be the best dye for mordant printing.

Finishing and Cleaning the Background

After the textile has been dyed in an immersion bath, it should be thoroughly rinsed and boiled by using a neutral detergent to remove any excess dye. Boiling with wheat bran will remove staining from the background. If any staining remains after the boiling, it will usually fade quickly once the textile is exposed to light.

Refer to chapter 9, "Finishing of Dyed and Printed Textiles."

To see samples of various dyes with the printed mordants, refer to the appendix, pages 169–170.

The traditional approach to cleaning the background of printed textiles, after boiling, was to lay the textiles on the ground, where they were bleached by the presence of moisture and ozone.

89

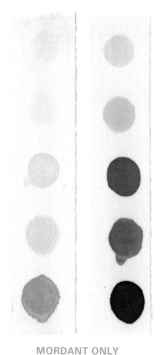

Mordants for printing, no tannin. Aluminum acetate and ferrous acetate combinations applied to cotton, dyed with weld.

Mordants for printing, treated with tannin. Aluminum acetate and ferrous acetate combinations applied to tannin-treated cotton, dyed with weld. If a textile has been treated with tannin, any mordant containing iron will immediately turn very dark and affect all subsequent dyeing.

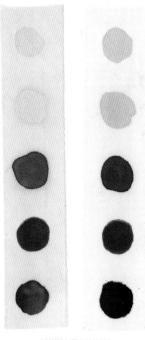

MORDANT ONLY

WITH TANNIN

ALUMINUM ACETATE

WELD

MADDER

Top: printed aluminum acetate mordant, bottom: printed ferrous acetate mordant. Dyed with weld and madder. Aluminum acetate is mixed with a very small amount of brazilwood extract in order to be visible on the textile.

FERROUS ACETATE

Ferrous acetate mordant printed on cotton over tannin, dye, or both: A. strong gallnut tannin, B. weak tannic acid, C. weld dye, D. madder dye. Once the mordant has been printed, a permanent bond is made with the tannin or dye. The fabric is dried and only rinsing/washing is necessary.

Mordant printing on silk, dyed with madder. Although no mordant is present in the background, most dyes will attach to the background of a printed silk textile, and it is impossible to remove.

DISCHARGE OF THE MORDANT

Mordant discharge is the removal of mordant by the use of an acid. It is frequently used to achieve a reverse pattern on a dyed ground. The mordant is first applied to the entire textile. Thickened citric acid is then used to selectively discharge the mordant. The discharge paste can be applied with any printing technique. The acid dissolves the metal oxides formed in the fibers. The mordant attaches to the acid and rinses out in the dunging process.

Apply the discharge paste to the acetate mordants, after the mordant is dry but before it has been dunged. This will completely remove the mordant. To some extent, it is possible to discharge previously dyed textiles, but once the mordant and dye are bound together they are more difficult to remove.

With care, mordant discharge can be used on all textiles. Always dung the textile in a chalk solution after discharge to neutralize any remaining citric acid. If not removed, the acid will damage the fiber.

🌿 Refer to recipe 26.

A citric-acid solution can be used to clean iron stains from dye vessels or studio glass wear. Cleansers that contain oxalic acid are also effective. The acid binds to the iron, in the same way that it binds to the iron mordant when discharging.

Mordant discharge: A. ferrous acetate mordant, discharged with citric acid, B. ferrous acetate mordant, discharged and dyed, C. aluminum acetate mordant, discharged and dyed, D. ferrous acetate, discharged, with additional application of aluminum acetate mordant after drying and dunging. All samples are dyed by using cochineal.

Printing

DIRECT PRINTING OF DYE AND MORDANT

While the "dyed style" can produce various shades and tones from a single dye, the direct application of dye makes it possible to apply several different dyes onto the same textile. Direct printing is appropriate for cotton, silk, or lightweight wool. A concentrated dye solution is mixed with a mordant, a thickener, and a weak acid. The presence of the acid prevents the lake from forming while the dye is in solution. After application, the dye and mordant will form a lake in the textile, but only after the acid has evaporated or been neutralized. Drying will cause some of the acid to evaporate. Steaming further ensures that the evaporation is complete, and helps the dye penetrate into the textile. Dunging ensures that any remaining vinegar is neutralized.

Direct application requires the use of concentrated dye solutions. Use either dye extracts or very strong dye extractions made from dye source material. Our approach to direct application of dye and mordant is based on old industrial recipes for printing with natural dyes.

Dyes that are printed directly exhibit slightly less vibrancy, depth of color, and lightfastness than those applied by mordant printing. The thickening agents used in the dye paste will bind to a small portion of the printed dyestuff, making it unavailable to the textile. Increased use of thickening agents will cause less dye to attach to the textile. An application of tannin prior to printing with the dyes or afterward will significantly improve lightfastness.

Refer to recipe 27 and 28.

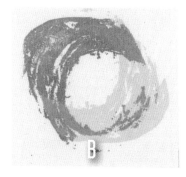

Direct application of dye paste and mordant (weld and madder) screened on to textile: A. before steaming, B. after steaming.

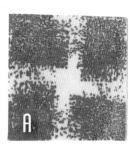
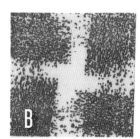
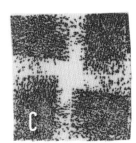
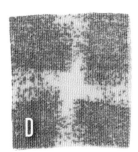

Direct printing of madder dye paste with mordant on cotton (A.), cotton treated with tannin (B.), silk (C.), lightweight wool (D.).

Space-Dyed Yarns with Multiple Mordants or Dye Colors

The techniques of mordant printing and direct application of dyes can be adapted for use on yarns in order to create "space-dyed" effects. The mordants and dyes are applied, without thickeners, so that they will blend together and penetrate into the yarns, usually with no undyed background areas remaining.

Apply unthickened acetate mordants to cellulose yarns. Dry and dung the mordants and dye the yarn in an immersion dye bath. The result will be various shades of a single dye color.

Direct application is used to achieve multiple colors on protein or cellulose yarns. If an overall dye coverage is intended (with no white or undyed places), the yarn can be pre-mordanted, followed by the application of concentrated dye solutions without thickeners, or acid. The dye colors will bleed together, mixing on the yarns. Steam the yarn immediately to ensure that the dye completely penetrates the yarns.

If white or undyed areas are desired, do not pre-mordant the yarn. Mix the concentrated dye solutions with vinegar and mordant but do not thicken. Steam the yarn immediately.

Finish the yarn with a thorough rinsing, as described in chapter 9.

"Space-dyed effect" on cotton yarn with mordant application: aluminum and ferrous acetate mordants, applied without thickener, to cotton yarn. After drying and dunging, each skein was dyed with a single dye: weld, cochineal, and madder.

Direct application of dye applied to pre-mordanted wool and cotton yarn. Concentrated dyes, without thickeners, were applied, and the yarn was steamed immediately.

93

Pigments and Dye Lakes

Pigments are insoluble and cannot be used as such to dye textiles. They can be applied directly to a textile or other substrate by the use of a binder. Natural pigments include ochers, indigo, Maya blue, and dye lakes. The preferred natural binder for textiles is freshly made soy milk. Soy milk contains proteins that coagulate and act as binder. It has little effect on the hand of the textile.

Ochers are natural earth pigments that are primarily iron oxides. They are mined, washed, ground, and sometimes heated to high temperatures to develop richer tones of orange, red, or brown. Earth pigments are sourced from around the world.

Extracted indigo powder is a pigment until it has been reduced in a vat, where it becomes a dye. When applied as a pigment, it is a dark, dull blue.

Maya blue is a brilliant turquoise-colored pigment made from indigo. It was an important colorant used by pre-Columbian Mayan and Aztec cultures and is famous for its resistance to aging and weathering. Michel Garcia has developed a method of making this pigment in the studio by mixing indigo with a particular type of mineral clay. The clay has a very open structure with long, interior channels. When heated with a small amount of indigo, the dye sublimates (moves directly from a solid to a gas) into the channels of the clay. The result is a stable pigment of brilliant turquoise color.

A **dye lake** is a pigment that is usually made from a leftover dye bath through recycling. It is in the form of a paste (recipe 16).

The ochers, indigo pigment, and Maya blue are all extremely lightfast and are excellent choices for textile artwork that will be hung on the wall and exposed to light. Pigments made from mordant dyes exhibit the same lightfastness qualities as the original dye material. All these pigments can be mixed to extend the palette.

When pigments are applied to the textile, their attachment is only as good as the binder that is used. These textiles are not as washfast as those that are dyed, and care should be used not to wash or rub them aggressively.

Refer to recipe 16, 29, 30, and 31.

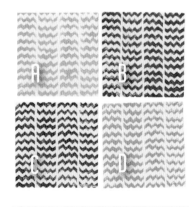

A. Maya blue, B. indigo, C. cochineal dye lake, D. yellow ocher pigments applied by using a printing block on soy-treated cotton.

Shades of green that result from mixing Maya blue and natural yellow ocher.

Red ocher applied to cotton over clay indigo resist paste.

Indigo Printing

There are several printing applications that can be used in combination with indigo.

- Resist pastes, made of natural materials, are used to prevent the dye from reaching all areas of a textile when it is dyed in indigo.
- An alkaline indigo paste, printed directly on the textile, allows the reduction to be made without the use of an immersion vat.
- Discharge of indigo by using oxidation.

INDIGO RESIST PASTE

"Blue printing" or "blue calico" are terms used to describe blue-and-white textiles that use a paste resist to restrict the indigo from reaching specified areas. The resist pastes usually contain both a chemical agent to precipitate the leuco indigo and a mechanical agent to prevent the dye from penetrating into the fibers, by forming a dense barrier layer on the surface of the textile.

Historically, these agents might have included lead acetate or nitrate of copper as chemical agents. Soy pastes, rice pastes, resins, or waxes were used as mechanical agents. A fatty substance was frequently added to make the paste easier to apply by using printing blocks or stencils.

Michel Garcia has shared a clay-based paste for indigo resist, using ingredients that are benign and easy to obtain. The paste includes clay, magnesium sulfate, and gum arabic.

- Clay is used to expand and physically fill the spaces of the textile in order to form a resist, forming a physical barrier. We recommend using finely ground clays such as bentonite and kaolin.

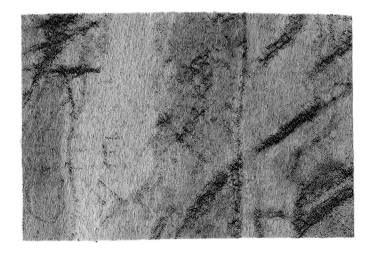

Maya blue, natural ochers, and lake pigments, when combined, will result in a full palette of pigment colors. *Woven and painted textile by Bethanne Knudson*.

- Magnesium sulfate or Epsom salts [$MgSO_4$] are used as the chemical resist. If the dye penetrates beyond the physical barrier of the clay, the magnesium reacts with the leuco indigo and the indigo will become insoluble. Magnesium sulfate has no color and is completely benign.
- Gum arabic is a natural gum made from hardened sap of the acacia tree. It is used to thicken the paste and help it attach.

The paste dissolves easily in water after dyeing is complete.

Refer to recipe 32.

A different type of indigo resist is made in China by using equal amounts of soybean powder and lime (calcium hydroxide). The paste holds up well in the vat but does not dissolve as easily during the rinsing. For this reason it is a suitable resist for use with the indigo discharge solution.

Refer to recipe 33.

Clay resist paste applied with silkscreen (A.), printing block (B.), brush (C.). All dyed in a single 12-minute indigo immersion.

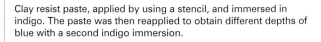

Clay resist paste, applied by using a stencil, and immersed in indigo. The paste was then reapplied to obtain different depths of blue with a second indigo immersion.

A single application of clay resist paste on cotton, immersed in dye vat 1, 2, 3, or 4 times. The paste was dried between each 10-minute immersion but was not reapplied. As the paste begins to break down, the dye is able to penetrate farther and reach the cloth.

DIRECT PRINTING WITH INDIGO

Indigo dye must be reduced in order to become soluble and dye a textile. This makes direct application of the dye challenging. One approach is to mix a small, very concentrated indigo vat. A brush, dipped into the concentrated vat, is used to apply the indigo to a textile. If done quickly, some of the dye will transfer, but much of it will oxidize during the transfer and become insoluble before it ever reaches the textile. This is not an effective method to achieve deep indigo colors or for controlled printing.

A more effective approach to indigo printing onto cellulose is derived from a former industrial practice. This method requires that the reduction material, in this case sugar, be applied directly to the textile. When the sugar combines with an alkaline indigo print paste, the reduction will occur in the textile itself during steaming. The indigo dissolves and the result is a true indigo-dyed print.

This approach to indigo printing was also used for discharge printing on cotton textiles dyed with madder or weld. The strong alkaline paste removes the mordant dye during the steaming, replacing it with indigo blue. The alkaline paste can also be used without the indigo as a clear discharge, removing the mordant and the dye. Various shades of indigo blue can be achieved by varying the amount of dye in the paste.

🌿 Refer to recipe 34.

Direct printing of indigo dye with alkaline paste: A. on white linen, B. on madder-dyed linen, C. on weld-dyed linen. The discharge spreads beyond the indigo print, creating a "halo" effect.

 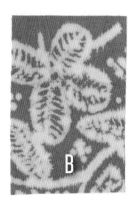

A. Direct print of light-blue indigo paste on madder-dyed cloth. B. Direct print with alkaline paste without indigo added.

DISCHARGE OF INDIGO BY USING OXIDATION (POTASSIUM PERMANGANATE)

Potassium permanganate [$KMnO_4$] is a potassium salt of manganese and is an oxidation agent. It is a deep-purple crystal and is used medicinally for wound care and also for water filtration. Once in contact with indigo, it breaks down the indigo, and the potassium permanganate is converted to brown manganese dioxide. When the textile is immersed in a citric-acid solution, the manganese dioxide dissolves and binds to the acid. This is similar to the way citric acid dissolves and binds metal mordants. Once the indigo and manganese are removed, the resulting textile is white or near white. It is suitable for cellulose or silk.

The potassium permanganate solution is used only as an immersion bath. If thickened with gum, the gum would convert the potassium permanganate into manganese dioxide before it has a chance to break down the indigo, and, as a result, it would no longer be effective. The soy/lime indigo resist paste can be printed on the dyed textile as a resist for the discharge solution.

In addition to discharging indigo, potassium permanganate can also be used as a source of a mineral brown color on cellulose, as referred to in *The Art and Craft of Natural Dyeing* by Jim Liles. Instead of removing the manganese dioxide by using a citric-acid solution, the textile is treated with a reducing sugar solution. The sugar halts the oxidizing effect of the permanganate and eliminates the deteriorating effects of the permanganate on the cellulose textile. The result is a permanent light-brown color from manganese dioxide. If the textile has been previously treated with tannin, the brown deepens as a result of the mineral combining with the tannin. The mineral brown is recommended only for cellulose.

Indigo on silk can be discharged when the citric acid removes the manganese dioxide, but it should not be treated with sugar, since the manganese dioxide would then remain in the textile and potentially damage it when exposed to UV light, similar to the effect of iron.

Manganese exists in nature and is considered benign, like iron.

Refer to recipe 35 and 36.

Discharge of indigo dye on cotton with potassium permanganate: A. original indigo-dyed fabric, B. discharged and finished with citric acid, C. discharged and finished with reducing sugar, D. indigo-dyed cloth, treated with tannin, discharged, and finished with reducing sugar.

Use of discharge on folded and clamped resist textiles: A. clamp resist with traditional indigo dye on white textile, B. dyed with indigo, resisted and discharged, C. dyed with indigo, resisted, discharged, and treated with reducing sugar, D. dyed with indigo, treated with tannin, resisted, discharged, and treated with reducing sugar.

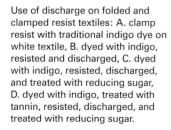

Soy lime paste printed on the indigo-dyed textile to resist the potassium permanganate discharge: A. cotton, discharged, treated with citric acid, B. cotton, discharged, treated with reducing sugar, C. cotton, discharged, treated with tannin and reducing sugar on cotton, D. silk, treated with citric acid.

Combining Techniques

Multiple techniques may be combined in order to create a complex design on the textile. These might include, but are not limited to:

- Mordant printing
- Direct application of dyes
- Discharge of mordants
- Optional use of tannins
- Indigo immersion dyeing, with or without resists
- Indigo printing

The dyer might also experiment with textiles that have been previously mordanted and dyed by printing either indigo or an iron mordant on the surface.

If a dyed background is required in combination with direct application of dye and mordant, it is best to finish the printing and then mordant and overdye the entire textile.

Combining direct printing with immersion dyeing: A. first, print dye with mordant, then mordant and dye the entire textile, B. print mordant and dye on indigo-dyed textile.

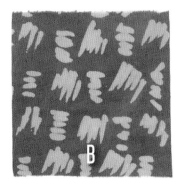

Ferrous acetate, applied to the whole textile, dried and discharged. The entire cloth was mordanted in concentrated aluminum acetate and dyed with weld. Deepest shades result from a combination of tannin and iron: A. no tannin, B. tannin added to weld dye bath, C. fabric tannined before initial application of ferrous acetate mordant.

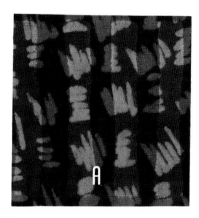
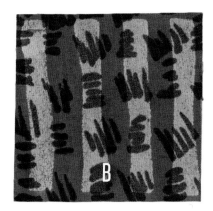
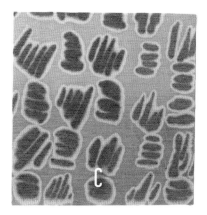

A. printed with resist paste and dyed with indigo, mordanted with aluminum acetate, printed mordant discharge, dyed with madder. B. printed with resist paste and dyed in indigo, printed directly with mordant and dye (madder). C. fabric was space dyed by using a direct application of dyes and mordant, then printed with indigo print paste.

A. indigo-dyed cotton, treated with tannin and printed with ferrous acetate. B. indigo-dyed cotton, printed with aluminum acetate, dyed with weld (green), and finally printed with ferrous acetate (black).

Finishing of Dyed and Printed Textiles

A ll dyed textiles must be cleaned thoroughly. At the very least, they should be washed by using a pH-neutral detergent and rinsed thoroughly until no dye comes off the fiber. Thorough and complete cleaning removes all excess dye from the surface and will further fix the dye in the fiber. This improves the clarity of the color and the fastness of the dye. Our recommendations for finishing are based on industrial processes and were used for all commercial finishing of naturally dyed textiles.

Immersion-Dyed Textiles

MORDANT DYES AND INDIGO

These are dyes that become insoluble in the textile. For this reason, they can be subjected to aggressive washing and rinsing.

All industrially dyed and printed textiles were "boiled" to finish them. Cottons textiles were boiled vigorously for approximately 10 minutes. Protein fibers were brought to a near simmer ($\approx$70°C/160°F for silk or $\approx$80°C/180°F for wool), and the temperature was maintained for 10 minutes.

During boiling, the fibers swell as a result of the water and the high temperature. The insoluble mordant dyes and indigo penetrate farther inside the fiber and combine into larger units. These larger dye units are better fixed in the textile and result in a slight change in hue, brightening the color.

- Excess dye on the surface of the textile is removed, improving the rubfastness.

- Larger dye units mean that not all dye molecules are subjected to equal exposure from light, improving the lightfastness.

Use a small amount of neutral detergent, such as Synthrapol™ or Orvus Paste™, in the final cleaning. Fat-based soaps are effective in absorbing excess indigo and other dyes in the finishing process, but their high alkalinity will damage mordants or fiber. Marseille soap is a mild olive oil soap (pH 8.0–9.0). Traditionally, it was used for finishing of cotton textiles in France. Marseille soap may be used to finish cellulose fiber, but do not use a fat-based soap unless all dyeing is complete. The fat can prevent further take-up of dye or additional mordants. Rinse well after cleaning.

Chapter 9
Finishing of Dyed and Printed Textiles

DYES APPLIED WITHOUT MORDANTS

The bond between dye and fiber, although strong, is soluble, and these dyes will not withstand vigorous washing or boiling. For this reason, dyes applied without mordants, including one-bath acid dyes, cannot be overdyed in a heated dye bath. Wash the textiles in lukewarm water with a small amount of neutral detergent. Rinse until clear.

Printed Textiles

MORDANT-PRINTED TEXTILES

Mordant-printed textiles should be cleaned in the same manner as any mordant-dyed textile. The unmordanted background will often "stain" with excess dye during the heated immersion bath, despite the fact that there is no mordant present.

The use of wheat bran is effective in removing the unwanted dye from the background. Place a handful of feed-grade wheat bran into a net bag. The bag will contain the bran and keeps particles from adhering to the textile as it boils with the bran in water for 10 minutes. The bran has an affinity for the dye and will draw it out of the nonmordanted background. Any residual staining of the background will often fade quickly once the textile is exposed to light.

BEFORE   AFTER

TEXTILES PRINTED WITH DYE AND MORDANT

Boil cellulose textiles in water with detergent to finish. Heat silk or wool to an appropriate temperature (≈70°C/160°F for silk or ≈80°C/180°F for wool) by using a small amount of neutral detergent. This is especially important with textiles that have not been subjected to a heated immersion dye bath. Excess dye is removed from the surface, the color becomes clearer, and the rubbing fastness will be greatly improved.

Mordant printing on cotton, immersion dyed with madder and weld, before and after cleaning in bran scour.

CHAPTER 10
Dye Fastness

There are many naturally dyed textiles that have survived for centuries. The dyes have endured as a result of the dye choices and the skill of the dyer. This chapter defines the various types of "fastness" and how to test for them.

Lightfastness

All dyes will fade over time as textiles are exposed to UV light. This is true of synthetic dyes as well as natural dyes. Some dyes fade very quickly while others fade more slowly and gradually. Some dyes lighten to pleasing shades that are less intense versions of the original color. Others become unattractive hues that are unrelated to the original dye color. There are some dyes that disappear almost completely, though many of these are often not considered true "dyes" but, instead, temporary "stains." The best dyes are those that fade slowly, evenly, and predictably and produce pleasing hues. Textile fibers themselves break down over time and with exposure to light. Ideally the color should last as long as the textile.

As stated earlier, most sources of natural dye contain more than one dye. Some of the dye constituents within a source material are more lightfast than others, so that the tone of the color may shift over time. Tannins often deepen when exposed to UV light, and dyes that contain tannin may darken or turn brownish.

Ramie, dyed with madder. One-half of samples were exposed to sunlight for 3 weeks: A. mordant only, B. tannin and mordant, C. post-mordanted with iron.

Chapter 10
Dye Fastness

When combining more than one dye in a textile, it is best to select dyes that have a similar lightfastness so that the balance of the color in the textile remains the same. Fibers have different absorption characteristics for UV light. Wool fiber has the capacity to absorb more UV light than any other natural fiber, which in turn protects the dyes from the UV light. This generally results in better lightfastness on wool than on silk or cellulose. Consequently, the same dye may exhibit better lightfastness on wool than on other fibers. Tannins will increase the lightfastness of all dyes, including indigo, by absorbing UV light and protecting the fiber.

Darker colors are more lightfast than paler ones from the same dye because the density created by additional dye molecules prevents the light from reaching all the dye molecules. Very small amounts of iron will increase the lightfastness of most dyes as well.

Cochineal on wool at different strengths (1–20% w.o.f.). One-half of samples were exposed to direct sunlight for 3 weeks.

Indigo: 1, 2, and 3 dips in the vat. One-half of samples were exposed to direct sunlight for 3 weeks.

The intended use of a textile may influence the dyes that are chosen. When making artwork that is to be hung on the wall, very careful decisions must be made regarding dye choice. A scarf that sits in a drawer most of the time will not be exposed to much light. In that case, a dye may be acceptable that would not be suitable for a household textile.

There are industry standards for measuring lightfastness of textiles. The two standards in use are the International Organization for Standardization (ISO) standard and the American Society for Testing Materials (ASTM) standard.

The ISO standard quantifies lightfast levels from 1 (fugitive) to 8 (extremely lightfast). The ASTM scale ranges from V (fugitive) to I (extremely lightfast). The difference between each level in both scales is significant, as shown in the following chart.

COMPARISON OF ISO AND ASTM LIGHTFAST LEVELS			
ISO	Megalux hours*	ASTM	Normal conditions indoor, indirect light
8	900	I	Excellent lightfastness, the color will remain unchanged for more than 100 years
7	300		
6	100	II	Very good lightfastness, unchanged for 50 – 100 years
5	32	III	Fair lightfastness, unchanged for 15 – 50 years
4	10		
3	3.6	IV	Poor lightfastness, begins to fade in 2 – 15 years
2	1.3		
1	0.4	V	Very poor lightfastness, begins to fade in 2 years or less

(Colby 1992)
Megalux hours refer to the number of exposure hours before fading becomes noticeable. Exposure to average indirect indoor lighting (120–180 lux) for an average of 12 hours a day equals 0.53–0.79 Megalux hours each year.

Dye Fastness

The recommendation for apparel textiles is ISO 4.0–4.5. The contract standard for interior textiles is 5.5–6.0. The best natural dyes range from 4.0 to 6.0. A dye that exhibits a lightfast level lower than 4 is considered unacceptable for most purposes.

For comparison, fiber-reactive dyes have lightfast levels ranging from 4 to 7 in full shade, depending on the dye color selected. Indigo, when dyed with long dips in a well-reduced vat, has a lightfastness level of ≈ 4.5. Greatly diminished lightfastness will result from short dips in the indigo vat or from a vat that is not well reduced.

Mixing two different dyes with excellent lightfastness is recommended as an alternative to using a single dye with poor lightfastness. For instance, Osage orange, a warm yellow dye, exhibits a poor lightfastness. A nearly identical color can be achieved by mixing weld, which has excellent lightfastness, with a very small amount of madder.

Logwood is initially a very attractive dye, but the clear, deep-purple color is extremely fugitive, fading to an unattractive brown tone. Historically, logwood was widely used to achieve black colors, but in general it was disallowed by the dye guilds because of its fugitive nature. A far more stable purple, similar to the color achieved from logwood, can be achieved by using a combination of cochineal and indigo.

ISO STANDARD BLUE WOOL LIGHTFASTNESS SCALE

Lightfastness can be measured and documented accurately, even in a small dye studio. The ISO scale consists of eight blue wool samples, which are affixed to a small card. Each blue color has been dyed with a different dye, carefully formulated to fade at a very specific rate from exposure to light. The blue-scale textile-fading cards are available for purchase from archival supply sources.

To use the scale, cover one side of the test card and one-half of the dye samples to be tested, using an opaque card. Place both the test card and the dye samples in a window and keep a record of the start date. The light that falls on the samples may be direct for a faster test or indirect for a slower test. Industry uses a xenon arc light, which has very high UV concentration, to speed up the process.

The first blue wool increment to fade indicates a lightfast level of 1.0. If a dyed sample fades at a similar rate as the first blue wool, it also has a lightfastness level of "1.0." This is very fugitive and is considered unacceptable for any dyed textile. After continued exposure to light, the second blue wool will fade. Again, if the dyed textile fades at the same rate, then the lightfast level is "2.0." Continued exposure to light will result in each of the levels of blue wool fading. The length of time between each of these increments is dependent on the intensity of light and the amount of UV exposure.

Interpreting the lightfastness test requires careful observation. This test is an excellent way to be objective about the dyes being used. A single blue-wool card can be used to test a number of samples simultaneously. With practice, the dyer will begin to get a sense of how long a color needs to be in the window to reach a lightfast level of 4.0 or 5.0.

The results of the blue-wool chart and lightfast tests illustrated in photos on the top half of page 107 can be compared. Weld exhibits a lightfastness of ≈ 5. The dyed sample has not yet begun to fade, nor has the no. 5 wool sample. Cutch is similar to no. 4, while madder and cochineal are closer to no. 3. Logwood exhibits a lightfastness of ≈ 1, while Osage is $\approx 1-2$ and brazilwood is ≈ 2. All the cotton samples were treated with tannin and aluminum acetate mordants. Wool always exhibits a greater lightfastness than cotton.

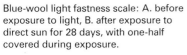

A

B

Blue-wool light fastness scale: A. before exposure to light, B. after exposure to direct sun for 28 days, with one-half covered during exposure.

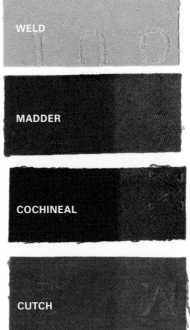

WELD

MADDER

COCHINEAL

CUTCH

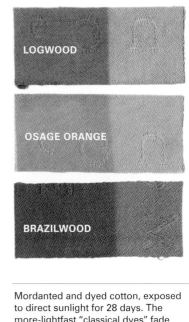

LOGWOOD

OSAGE ORANGE

BRAZILWOOD

Mordanted and dyed cotton, exposed to direct sunlight for 28 days. The more-lightfast "classical dyes" fade vsomewhat yet still maintain integrity of color, while the less successful dyes fade to colors that bear little resemblance to the original.

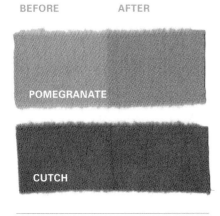

BEFORE   AFTER

POMEGRANATE

CUTCH

Pomegranate and cutch dyes on wool, exposed to direct sun for 21 days. The tannins will oxidize and darken when exposed to UV light, while some of the flavonoids will fade.

BEFORE   AFTER

LOGWOOD

INDIGO + COCHINEAL

BEFORE   AFTER

OSAGE ORANGE

WELD + MADDER

A. logwood dye compared to indigo/cochineal combination, on silk, B. Osage orange dye compared to weld/madder combination on wool. All samples were exposed to direct sunlight for 3 weeks.

107

Dye Fastness

Rubfastness

Poor finishing, insufficient mordant, or an excess of dye can all result in color that will rub from the surface of the textile. The fixation of the dye in the fiber can be tested by using a rubfast test. Place a small piece of dry, white, cotton cloth on the finger and vigorously rub the surface of the dyed textile. If color comes off onto the white cloth, it is not resistant to rubbing and might rub off onto other textiles or the body. This is a common problem with indigo, particularly when it sits on the surface of the textile as a result of insufficient finishing.

Washfastness

Good mordanting and finishing of textiles will result in dyes that resist washing out. Excess dye must be removed from the fiber during the finishing process or it will come off, especially during the first washing.

Perspiration

Perspiration can be either acid or alkaline, and both of these can have an effect on the dye/mordant. Extremely acidic perspiration might remove some dye and mordants. Dyes such as cochineal and lac are particularly sensitive to pH changes, and the color shifts slightly.

Care of Naturally Dyed Textiles

Naturally dyed textiles are unique products and, like any fine textile, should only receive handwashing or gentle machine washing in cool water, followed by line drying. Careful cleaning will make a textile (and dye) last longer. Some dyes are especially sensitive to changes in pH. Mordants and dyes are sensitive to some dry-cleaning fluids or to the use of strong alkaline soaps. Only a mild, neutral detergent should be used for washing naturally dyed textiles.

Strong acids such as lemon juice, or even lemonade, can damage naturally dyed textiles. If accidently spilled onto a textile, the acid will remove the mordant and the dye. The best way to treat a spill is to flush the textile immediately with a large amount of cold water. The acid will be removed, but some of the mordant will remain and will reattach to the dye in the textile.

In general, the use of fabric softeners is not recommended. They soften the textile by lubricating the surface of the fibers with a very thin layer of an oily substance, which reduces friction between the yarns and the fibers. Fabric softeners are not environmentally friendly.

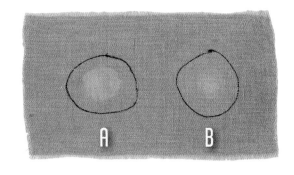

A. Lemonade was dripped onto the textile and left to dry, removing the mordant and dye. B. Textile was flushed in cold water immediately after the spill, preserving most of the mordant and dye.

CHAPTER 11
Recipes

PRINCIPLES OF THE DYE KITCHEN

Labeling and Record Keeping

Whether performing dye tests or executing production dyeing, the dyer should always label textiles carefully. When sampling, write directly onto the textile with a permanent fabric-marking pen, or attach a small piece of cotton cloth or Tyvek® with a needle and thread or by using a tagging gun. Always test the marking pen carefully before use to be sure that it does not bleed or disappear!

Thoroughly document all processes, recipes, and samples. A dyer's log is the most valuable tool in the studio.

Safety

Always use a mask when measuring lightweight powders, to prevent irritation. Wear gloves to protect the skin. Be aware that some people are especially sensitive to chemical or plant substances.

Use only dedicated tools and equipment for all dyeing projects. Never use food preparation spaces or tools for dyeing or dye preparation.

Weights and Measures

The recipes in this book are written using the metric system of measurement for both dry and liquid ingredients. Both centigrade and Fahrenheit temperatures are included in all recipes.

Solids and all dry ingredients are measured by weight. A scale must have the capacity to weigh the quantities commonly used by the dyer; digital scales are the most accurate. Many kitchen scales will weigh appropriate quantities of dyes, chemicals, and fiber. For very small amounts or for greatest accuracy, obtain a jeweler's scale or use standard stock solutions as explained below.

- 1 g = 1 gram
- 1 kg = 1 kilogram = 1000 grams

Liquids are generally also weighed but can be measured by volume if specifically asked for in the recipe. When measuring clean, cool water (≈20°C/68°F), the volume (in milliliters) and the

Recipes

weight (in grams) are equivalent in the metric system (1 ml cool clean water = 1 g). This is not the case with any other liquid. All chemical solutions have a different ratio between volume and weight (density).

- 1 ml = 1 milliliter

- 1 L = 1 liter = 1000 ml

All dye and mordant formulas are based on the weight of a clean, dry textile.

- Weight of fiber (textile) = w.o.f. For instance, 1 percent w.o.f. equals 1 g per 100 g dry textile.

Making Solutions

Many recipes require the making of accurate solutions of mordants and other chemicals. To achieve the correct concentration, each chemical ingredient is weighed. The recipes indicate the amount of water either by weight or by stating "enough to attain total volume."

The chemical material in the solution must be thoroughly mixed to ensure a true dilution. Make solutions with warm water to help dissolve dry ing-

redients. Boiling water may be called in some recipes to ensure that materials are completely dissolved.

Standard stock solutions of dyes or chemicals for very small amounts are normally made as solutions that equal 1 g dye or chemical per 100 ml of solution. One ml of this solution contains 0.01 g of dye or chemical. Appropriate amounts can be measured by using a pipette, disposable syringe, or graduated cylinder.

Liquid Measure

Straight-sided transparent vessels such as beakers, graduated cylinders, and disposable syringes measure liquids with the greatest accuracy. These are available in plastic or glass and in a range of sizes from scientific, dye supply, or hobby suppliers. If a recipe calls for weights, even liquids must be weighed.

Temperature

Use thermometers for measuring the temperature of mordant and dye baths. All temperatures are given in Celsius and Fahrenheit.

pH

Determine acidity or alkalinity (the pH) of solutions by using either pH strips or a pH meter. A pH meter is more accurate, but it must be calibrated before each use by using a standard solution in order to assure its accuracy.

Vessels for Dyeing

Dyeing requires nonreactive pots. The best investment for the dyer is a variety of good-quality, food-grade, stainless steel pots. Unheated mordants can be accomplished in plastic vessels.

Aluminum pots are not suitable for mordanting or dyeing. The surface of the pot will pit and deteriorate when exposed to water, acids, mordants, tannins, and some dyes. Occasionally, the dyer can make use of an iron, copper, or brass pot to allow small amounts of mordants to leach from the metal as a color modifier.

The textile should be kept completely immersed in the dye bath while dyeing. A tall narrow pot is preferable to a wide shallow one (which will have a greater surface area). If allowed to rise above the surface of the bath, the textile will not dye evenly or well.

A flat, stainless steel grid or rack, placed a short distance from the bottom, will prevent the textile from touching the very hot bottom surface of the pot.

Liquid Volume for Mordanting and Dyeing

The amount of liquid volume in a mordant or dye bath is not critical from a chemical perspective; both mordant and dye will find their way to the textile. The amount of liquid in the bath is critical in terms of ensuring that there is sufficient volume for uniform dyeing. The textile must be evenly exposed to the dye bath, with ample room to move around. It is more difficult to attain an even dye on fabric than on yarn because of a fabric's tendency to float and fold. For this reason, fabric requires more liquid in the dye pot than do yarns of equal weight. Liquor ratio describes the weight of the textile to the weight of the liquid bath and may range from 1 part of textile weight to 30–50 parts of water volume (1:30–1:50).

The one exception is a tannin bath. When tannin is applied to cellulose prior to mordanting, the bath is an equilibrium, which means that the tannin in the bath is in balance with the tannin in the textile. If too much water is used, it may decrease the amount of tannin that attaches to the fibers.

Recipes

Water

Do not underestimate the importance of the specific characteristics of water. The quality of water used for mordanting and dyeing will affect the final results. Water from different sources can produce very different colors.

Water can contain varying amounts of metals or calcium, depending on its source and location. Soft water is slightly acidic and has the capacity to dissolve metals from the soil or from metal pipes. When acidic water stands for a long time in metal pipes, it can absorb considerable amounts of iron, copper, or other metals that may be present in the pipes. The presence of these metal ions in the water will act as a mordant, and the colors will be affected.

Acidic water will also leach minerals from iron, brass, or copper pots. When the acidity of the water is slightly increased, the ability of the water to dissolve the mineral mordants in the metal is also increased.

Hard water, which contains calcium, is likely to be alkaline. Calcium is beneficial for fixing some dyes, such as weld and madder, but not suitable for others, such as cochineal or lac. Most other dyes will not be adversely affected by the use of hard water. Sometimes a small amount of chalk (calcium carbonate) is added to a madder or weld dye bath, in order to neutralize acidic water and brighten the dye colors.

Understand your water and its source. Measure the pH. Test the water for trace amounts of iron by adding a pinch of gallic tannin to a small amount of water. If the water turns gray or black, iron is likely present. The amount of calcium in hard water can be determined by using commercially available calcium test strips.

Water that contains iron is especially problematic for the dyer. Brilliant, clear colors can never be achieved if the water contains iron. It is best to consult with a professional to determine the amount of iron present and the treatment. Ion exchange units will remove iron and soften water. Other options include gathering rainwater or using distilled water. Do not use chemical water softeners for dyeing.

THE RECIPES

The recipes are recommendations based on multiple tests and objective results. In some cases, more than one recipe has been included for a specific mordant or process, and the dyer may choose one or the other based on available ingredients, process, or cost.

Recipes

Cleaning (Pretreatment)

Recipes for cleaning textiles call for the use of a neutral or slightly acidic detergent, such as Orvus Paste®, Synthrapol®, or a neutral dishwashing liquid.

RECIPE 1

HOW TO CLEAN WOOL

This recipe is intended to remove spinning oils but is not suitable for removing dirt and grease from raw wool.

Ingredients:

- Neutral detergent at ≈1% w.o.f.

Procedure:

1. Fill a nonreactive pot of a size suitable for the textile with warm tap water. Allow enough room for the textile to float freely. Always leave enough room for the textile to be moved during the process.

2. Add the detergent.

3. Place the textile in the bath and immerse it completely.

4. Slowly increase the temperature to ≈60°C/140°F.

5. Maintain the temperature for approximately 1 hour.

6. Periodically, gently move the textile in the bath, making sure that it remains completely immersed at all times. Keep all movements gentle to avoid felting.

7. Cool the textile in the bath.

8. Rinse the wool carefully.

RECIPE 2

A SCOUR FOR CELLULOSE FIBERS

This recipe is intended to remove wax, dirt, and spinning oils from cellulose fibers.

Ingredients:

- Neutral detergent at ≈1% w.o.f.
- Soda ash at ≈1% w.o.f.

Procedure:

1. Fill a nonreactive pot of a size suitable for the textile with warm tap water. Allow enough room for the textile to float freely. Always leave enough room for the textile to be moved during the process.

2. Add the detergent and soda ash and stir until completely dissolved. The resultant solution should be at pH 8–9.

3. Place the textile in the bath and immerse it completely.

4. Slowly increase the temperature to a gentle boil (100°C/220°F).

5. Maintain the temperature for 1 to 2 hours.

6. Periodically move the textile in the bath, making sure that it remains completely immersed at all times. Add additional water, as needed, to maintain the liquid volume.

7. Cool the textile in the bath.

8. Rinse the textile thoroughly.

If the used scour bath is very dark or dirty, repeat the process.

Chapter 11

Recipes

RECIPE 3

WETTING OUT FOR WOOL, SILK, OR READY-TO-DYE (RTD) CELLULOSE TEXTILES

Use for textiles that are clean and only need to be wetted out before mordanting or dyeing.

Ingredients:
- Neutral detergent at ≈1% w.o.f.

Procedure:

1. Fill a nonreactive vessel of a size suitable for the textile with warm tap water. Allow enough room for the textile to float freely. Always leave enough room for the textile to be moved during the process.

2. Heat the water to ≈50°C/120°F unless tap water falls in this temperature range.

3. Add the detergent and stir until completely dissolved.

4. Place the textile in the bath and immerse it completely.

5. Allow the textile to sit in the bath until thoroughly wet. A fine silk may wet out in just a few minutes, while heavy, dense textiles may require several hours or overnight. Additional heat is not necessary, but gently heating the bath will decrease the time required for wetting out heavier or tightly constructed textiles. Wool that has been pre-mordanted and dried will take much longer to wet out than wool that has not been mordanted.

6. Rinse.

RECIPE 4

. . . .

A RECIPE FOR DEGUMMING SILK

Use only for removing sericin from silk.

Ingredients:
- Neutral detergent at ≈1% w.o.f.
- Soda ash at 10% w.o.f.
- White vinegar

Procedure:

1. Fill a nonreactive vessel of a size suitable for the textile with warm tap water. Allow enough room for the textile to float freely. Always leave enough room for the textile to be moved during the process.

2. Add the detergent and soda ash.

3. Warm the solution enough to allow the soda ash to dissolve completely.

4. Place the silk in the bath.

5. Slowly increase the temperature to just below a simmer to (≈90°C/195°F) and maintain the bath at that temperature for 30 to 60 minutes.

6. Rinse the sericin (which will be slimy) from the silk while the textile is still very warm, using warm water. Cold water can precipitate the sericin, making it more difficult to rinse out.

7. Neutralize the textile by immersing it in a sufficient quantity of a mild solution of white vinegar and water (approximately 15 ml vinegar per L water).

Recipes

Mordants for Immersion Dyeing

All mention of "alum" refers to potassium aluminum sulfate dodecahydrate [$KAl(SO_4)_2 12H_2O$].

Before mordanting, scour all textiles as needed and always wet out the textile completely prior to mordanting.

Mordants for Protein

RECIPE 5
. . . .

A TRADITIONAL HEATED ALUMINUM MORDANT FOR WOOL

Ingredients:
- Alum at 15% w.o.f.
- Cream of tartar at 5% w.o.f. (use only if required; refer to chapter 4)

Procedure:
1. Fill a nonreactive pot of a size suitable for the textile with warm tap water. Allow enough room for the textile to float freely. Always leave enough room for the textile to be moved during the process.
2. Add the alum and stir until completely dissolved.
3. Place the textile in the bath and immerse it completely.
4. Slowly increase the temperature to ≈90°C/195°F (just below a simmer).
5. Maintain the temperature of the bath for 1 hour.
6. Periodically, move the textile in the bath, making sure that it remains completely immersed at all times.
7. Allow the textile to cool in the pot.
8. Wearing gloves, squeeze the mordant liquid out of the textile. Save the mordant for reuse, if desired.
9. Rinse the textile well to ensure that any unattached mordant is removed from the surface of the textile.
10. Dye immediately or line dry the textile and store it for future dyeing.

RECIPE 6A

....

A "COLD" MORDANT PROCESS FOR WOOL

Wool can be mordanted without heat if a longer period of time is available. Heat accelerates the process but is not necessary. The mordant will penetrate into the textile if given enough time. This approach is very suitable for fragile wool yarns, such as merino, and will achieve results very similar to those using a traditional heated mordant bath.

Ingredients:
- Alum at 15–20% w.o.f.

Procedure:

1. Fill a nonreactive pot of a size suitable for the textile with warm tap water. Allow enough room for the textile to float freely. Always leave enough room for the textile to be moved during the process.

2. Add the alum and stir until completely dissolved.

3. Place the textile in the bath and immerse it completely.

4. Slowly increase the temperature to ≈90°C/195°F (just below a simmer).

5. Turn off the heat and allow the textile to sit in the mordant bath at room temperature for 24 hours.

6. Wearing gloves, squeeze the mordant liquid out of the textile. Save the mordant for reuse, if desired.

7. Rinse the textile well to ensure that any unattached mordant is removed from the surface of the textile.

8. Dye immediately or line dry the textile and store it for future dyeing.

Chapter 11
Recipes

RECIPE 6B
....

AN ALTERNATIVE "COLD" MORDANT PROCESS FOR WOOL

Ingredients:

- Alum at 15% w.o.f.

- Neutral detergent at ≈1% w.o.f. (this lowers the surface tension and ensures that the mordant penetrates the textile)

Procedure:

1. Fill a nonreactive pot of a size suitable for the textile with warm tap water. Allow enough room for the textile to float freely. Always leave enough room for the textile to be moved during the process.

2. Add the alum and detergent. Stir until completely dissolved.

3. Place the textile in the bath and immerse it completely.

4. Allow the textile to remain in the mordant for at least 4 days.

5. Wearing gloves, squeeze the mordant liquid out of the textile. Save the mordant for reuse, if desired.

6. Rinse the textile well to ensure that any unattached mordant is removed from the surface of the textile.

7. Dye immediately or line dry the textile and store it for future dyeing.

RECIPE 7

·················

A TIN MORDANT FOR WOOL

Ingredients:

- Tin (stannous chloride) at 3% w.o.f.
- Cream of tartar at 6% w.o.f.

Procedure:

1. Fill a nonreactive pot of a size suitable for the textile with warm tap water. Allow enough room for the textile to float freely. Always leave enough room for the textile to be moved during the process.

2. Add the tin and cream of tartar. Stir until completely dissolved.

3. Place the textile in the bath and immerse it completely.

4. Slowly increase the temperature to ≈90°C/195°F (just below a simmer).

5. Maintain the temperature of the bath for 1 hour.

6. Periodically, move the textile in the bath, making sure that it remains completely immersed at all times.

7. Allow the textile to cool in the pot.

8. Wearing gloves, squeeze the mordant liquid out of the textile. Save the mordant for reuse, if desired.

9. Rinse the textile well to ensure that any unattached mordant is removed from the surface of the textile.

10. Dye immediately or line dry the textile and store it for future dyeing.

Recipes

RECIPE 8

. . . .

AN ALUMINUM MORDANT FOR SILK

Always treat silk gently. Carefully squeeze excess mordants from the textile. Silk textiles should never be wrung out, since that has the potential of ripping delicate silks.

Ingredients:

- Alum at 15% w.o.f.

Procedure:

1. Fill a nonreactive pot of a size suitable for the textile with hot water ($\approx$60°C/140°F). Allow enough room for the textile to float freely. Always leave enough room for the textile to be moved during the process.

2. Add the alum. Stir until completely dissolved.

3. Place the textile in the bath and immerse it completely. Do not apply additional heat.

4. Allow the textile to sit in the mordant bath for 1 hour. It will cool to room temperature.

5. Periodically, move the textile in the bath, making sure that it remains completely immersed at all times.

6. Wearing gloves, gently squeeze the mordant liquid from the textile. Save the mordant for reuse, if desired.

7. Rinse the textile well to ensure that any unattached mordant is removed from the surface of the textile.

8. Dye immediately or line dry the textile and store it for future dyeing.

RECIPE 9

·················

AN ALTERNATIVE, CONCENTRATED ALUMINUM MORDANT FOR SILK

Ingredients:

Make a concentrated 5% solution with just enough volume to immerse the largest piece of textile. Use this recipe and scale up or down, as necessary.

Alum	50 g
Warm water (≈ 50°C/120°F)	950 g
Total	1000 g

Procedure:

1. Wearing rubber gloves, carefully immerse the silk in the mordant bath.

2. Move the textile in the bath to assure even application of mordant.

3. After 10 minutes, gently squeeze excess mordant from the textile back into the mordant vessel.

4. Rinse the textile well to ensure that any unattached mordant is removed from the surface of the textile.

5. Dye immediately or dry the textile and store for future dyeing.

···

NOTE: The remaining concentrated mordant bath can be used to mordant additional silk. Start with the largest pieces of textile/yarn and subsequently mordant smaller ones to ensure that no mordant is wasted. The remaining mordant solution can also be stored for future use.

Chapter 11

Recipes

RECIPE 10

A MIDDLE-MORDANT PROCESS FOR DYEING SILK

Ingredients:

- Alum at 15–20% w.o.f.

Preparation:

- Prepare a hot dye bath (≈85°C/185°F°) for the desired depth of shade based on w.o.f. Use enough water to allow the textile to float freely. When dyeing silk yarns or densely constructed textiles, the dyeing should be done by using a heated bath. Lightweight silk fabrics can be dyed in baths that have been brought up to temperature but then removed from the heat for the duration of the dyeing process.

- Prepare a room-temperature mordant bath with enough water for the textile to float freely.

Procedure:

1. Place the textile in the hot dye bath and immerse it completely. Allow it to remain in the dye for 10 minutes. Move the textile regularly. Wear heavy, insulated rubber gloves to protect hands from the heat.

2. Remove the textile from the dye bath, gently squeezing excess dye back into the bath. Do not rinse.

3. Place the textile into the mordant bath and immerse it completely. Allow it to remain in the mordant for 15 minutes. Move the textile regularly.

4. Remove the textile from the mordant bath.

5. Rinse well to remove any unattached mordant.

6. Place the textile back into the original hot dye bath for a second time. Move the textile regularly. After 10 minutes, remove the textile from the dye bath, gently squeezing excess dye back into the bath.

7. Rinse the textile well, and wash to finish.

NOTE: If additional layers of dye are desired, use a fresh dye bath and a fresh mordant bath.

Mordants for Cellulose

RECIPE 11

AN ALUMINUM MORDANT FOR IMMERSION DYEING OF CELLULOSE

NOTE: This is a two-step process. Step 1 is the application of tannin. Step 2 is the application of the mordant.

Step 1: Application of Tannin

Ingredients:

- Tannin extract (gall, sumac, tara, myrobalan) at 10% w.o.f.

- OR tannic acid at 20–30% w.o.f.

- OR ground tannin plant material at 20–30% w.o.f.

Procedure:

1. Fill a plastic or stainless steel vessel with hot water (≈40–50°C/100–120°F), using approximately a 30:1 (water:textile) ratio. There is an equilibrium between the amount of tannin on the fiber and the amount of tannin in the water. The success of the tannin bath is dependent on the correct amount of water and tannin.

2. Add the tannin and stir until dissolved or evenly distributed.

3. Place the textile in the bath and immerse it completely.

4. Soak the textile in the tannin bath for 1–2 hours, moving it occasionally to ensure even tannin penetration. The bath will cool during the process, and there is no need to reheat the bath. High temperatures will oxidize the tannin and potentially darken the textile.

5. Remove the textile from the tannin bath and, while wearing rubber gloves, squeeze excess back into the tannin bath. Save the tannin for reuse, if desired.

6. Rinse the tannin-soaked textile very lightly or, optionally, spin out excess tannin by using a centrifuge or washing machine. Tannin is bound to the fiber only by affinity and can be removed if rinsed too aggressively.

7. Mordant the textile immediately after the tannin step, while still damp. If the textile is allowed to dry and must be wet out again, some of the tannin will be lost.

8. The tannin application can be done with cold water, but the textile should then soak much longer, preferably overnight.

Step 2: Mordanting

Use one of the following recipes (11A–11D) for the aluminum mordant on cellulose. Each one is effective. Select the mordant of choice, based on available ingredients. All these mordants are applied by using an unheated process.

Recipes

RECIPE 11A

NEUTRAL ALUMINUM ACETATE (ALUMINUM TRIACETATE) [AL(C$_2$H$_3$O$_2$)$_3$]

Ingredients:

- Alum at 18% w.o.f.
- Sodium acetate at 16% w.o.f.

Procedure:

1. Fill a plastic or stainless steel vessel with enough warm water ($\approx$40–50°C/100–120°F) to immerse the textile. Allow room for the textile to move freely.

2. Add the alum and sodium acetate. Stir until completely dissolved.

3. Place the textile, which has been pretreated with tannin, into the mordant bath.

4. Allow the textile to sit in the mordant bath for 1 to 2 hours, stirring occasionally.

5. While wearing rubber gloves, remove the textile and squeeze excess mordant back into the bath. Save the mordant for reuse, if desired.

6. Rinse the textile well to ensure that any unattached mordant is removed from the surface of the textile.

7. The textile may be dyed immediately or dried for future dyeing.

NOTE: This recipe produces the equivalent of an 8 percent application of neutral aluminum acetate on the textile. When 18 g of alum combines with 16 g of sodium acetate, it produces 8 g of aluminum acetate. The remainder is byproducts of sodium sulfate (Glauber's salt), potassium sulfate, and water.

RECIPE 11B

······················

NEUTRAL ALUMINUM ACETATE (ALUMINUM TRIACETATE)

Ingredients:

- Alum at 18% w.o.f.

- White vinegar (5% acetic acid solution) at 240% w.o.f.

- Soda ash (sodium carbonate) at 10% w.o.f.

Procedure:

1. While stirring, mix together the alum, soda ash, and vinegar. Use a vessel that is twice the volume of the vinegar. The solution will bubble up as the alum and soda ash neutralize. The reaction is harmless and the bubbling will quickly subside, leaving a clear solution.

2. Add the mordant solution to a plastic or stainless steel vessel with enough warm water (≈40–50°C/100–120°F) to immerse the textile. Allow enough room for the textile to move freely.

3. Place the textile, which has been pretreated with tannin, into the mordant bath.

4. Allow the textile to sit in the mordant bath for 1 to 2 hours, stirring occasionally.

5. While wearing rubber gloves, remove the textile and squeeze excess mordant back into the bath. Save the mordant for reuse, if desired.

6. Rinse the textile well to ensure that any unattached mordant is removed from the surface of the textile.

7. The textile may be dyed immediately or dried for future dyeing.

Chapter 11
Recipes

RECIPE 11C
....

DIBASIC ALUMINUM ACETATE

Ingredients:
- Dibasic Aluminum acetate powder (also referred to as aluminum monoacetate) at 5% w.o.f.

Procedure:
1. Fill a plastic or stainless steel vessel with enough warm water ($\approx$40–50°C/100–120°F) to immerse the textile. Allow enough room for the textile to move freely.
2. Add the mordant. Stir until completely dissolved.
3. Place the textile, which has been pretreated with tannin, into the mordant bath.
4. Allow the textile to sit in the mordant bath for 1 to 2 hours, stirring occasionally.
5. While wearing rubber gloves, remove the textile and squeeze excess mordant back into the bath. Save the mordant for reuse, if desired.
6. Rinse the textile well to ensure that any unattached mordant is removed from the surface of the textile.
7. The textile may be dyed immediately or dried for future dyeing.

RECIPE 11D
....

MONOBASIC ALUMINUM ACETATE

Ingredients:

- Monobasic Aluminum acetate powder (also referred to as aluminum diacetate) at 6% w.o.f.

Procedure:

1. Fill a plastic or stainless steel vessel with enough warm water ($\approx$40–50°C/100–120°F) to immerse the textile. Allow enough room for the textile to move freely.

2. Add the mordant. Stir until completely dissolved.

3. Place the textile, which has been pretreated with tannin, into the mordant bath.

4. Allow the textile to sit in the mordant bath for 1 to 2 hours, stirring occasionally.

5. While wearing rubber gloves, remove the textile and squeeze excess mordant back into the bath. Save the mordant for reuse, if desired.

6. Rinse the textile well to ensure that any unattached mordant is removed from the surface of the textile.

7. The textile may be dyed immediately or dried for future dyeing.

Chapter 11

Recipes

RECIPE 11E

ALUM / SODA ASH MORDANT

Alum that is combined with a small amount of soda ash creates a compound similar to that used in Turkey red dyeing. It is an old recipe that was used industrially to mordant cellulose. It is the least expensive mordant and is equally effective as any of the aluminum acetate mordants. The recipe begins with two separate solutions: an alum solution and a soda ash solution. The amount of water in the solutions is not critical, but the solutions should be quite concentrated and allow for plenty of additional water to be added after they are combined.

Ingredients:

- Alum Solution: Alum at 12% w.o.f. Dissolve the alum in enough boiling water (approximately 200% of the fiber weight) to completely dissolve the alum. Allow the solution to cool.

- Soda Ash Solution: Soda ash at 1.5% w.o.f. Dissolve the soda ash in enough boiling water (approximately 200% of the fiber weight) to completely dissolve the soda ash. Allow the solution to cool.

Procedure:

1. Combine the alum solution and the soda ash solution while stirring. Bubbles will form and then quickly subside when these two solutions mix together, so be sure to use a large enough vessel to allow for this reaction.

2. Add additional warm water ($\approx$40–50°C/100–120°) as needed to allow the textile to be completely immersed.

3. Place the textile, which has been pretreated with tannin, into the mordant bath.

4. Allow the textile to sit in the mordant bath for 1 to 2 hours, stirring occasionally.

5. While wearing rubber gloves, remove the textile and squeeze excess mordant back into the bath. Save the mordant for reuse, if desired.

6. Rinse the textile well to ensure that any unattached mordant is removed from the surface of the textile.

7. The textile may be dyed immediately or dried for future dyeing.

Although it may appear that some of these recipes include more aluminum than others, they all produce an equivalent amount of aluminum deposit on the textiles and will produce very similar results from various aluminum compounds. Since each mordant performs similarly, the dyer has the flexibility to choose raw materials based on availability and cost, without compromising the results.

COMPARISON OF ALUMINUM MORDANTS FOR CELLULOSE

Recipe	Monobasic aluminum acetate	Dibasic aluminum acetate powder	Alum	Sodium acetate	Soda ash	Vinegar
11A. Aluminum acetate			18%	16%		
11B. Aluminum acetate			18%		10%	240%
11C. Dibasic aluminum acetate		5%				
11D. Monobasic aluminum acetate	6%					
11E. Alum/soda ash			12%		1.50%	

Recipes

RECIPE 12

....

CONCENTRATED ALUMINUM ACETATE WITHOUT TANNIN

Ingredients:

Alum	120 g
Sodium Acetate	100 g
Warm tap water	enough to attain total volume
Total	1000 ml

Procedure:

1. Mix only enough mordant solution to immerse the textile. This application does not require volume for the textile to move freely.

2. While wearing rubber gloves, immerse the prewetted textile in the mordant until it is completely saturated. This will take only about 3–5 minutes.

3. Remove the textile, squeezing excess mordant back into the container.

4. Without rinsing, dry the mordanted textile completely, either on a line or in a clothes dryer (using medium heat).

5. Dung the *dried* textile in a solution of chalk ($\approx$10 g calcium carbonate per L of hot water) until completely saturated. Rinse well in clear water.

6. To prevent waste of this concentrated mordant, first mordant the largest piece of textile and continue to mordant smaller pieces until the mordant has been completely used up. Any leftover mordant may be thickened for print applications.

....

NOTE: If the textile has been pretreated with tannin, drying and dunging is not necessary. Simply rinse excess mordant immediately and proceed to dyeing.

....

NOTE: Ferrous acetate mordant for printing (or any of the aluminum acetate / ferrous acetate mixtures) can also be applied by using this same process. Do not use the gum thickener.

Refer to recipe 23 and 24.

Post-dye Mordants—Applied after Aluminum Mordanting and Dyeing

When experimenting with iron, it is often helpful to reserve a small piece of the originally dyed textile so that it can be compared to the one that has been treated with iron.

RECIPE 13

IRON: FERROUS SULFATE (FOR WOOL AND CELLULOSE)

Ingredients:
- Ferrous sulfate at 1–2% w.o.f.

Procedure:

1. Fill a nonreactive pot with enough warm water to allow the textile to float freely. The water should be warm enough to dissolve the iron but not hot. ($\approx$60°C/140°F).

2. Add the ferrous sulfate and stir until completely dissolved.

3. Place the dyed, wetted-out textile into the bath. If applying to wool, increase the temperature to $\approx$70–80°C/160–180°F. When applying to cotton, there is no need to increase the temperature. Watch the textile carefully and remove it when the desired color is reached, keeping in mind that textiles always dry to a lighter shade than when wet. The iron attaches quickly and should take no longer than a few minutes.

4. Rinse and then wash the textile thoroughly to remove any unattached iron.

5. After using the dye vessel, scour it thoroughly to remove any iron residue.

Recipes

RECIPE 14

....

IRON: FERROUS ACETATE (FOR SILK AND CELLULOSE)

Use only ferrous acetate on silk. It can also be used on cellulose fiber and is likely to be less damaging to any textile than ferrous sulfate.

Ingredients:
- Ferrous sulfate at 1–2% w.o.f.
- Sodium acetate at 1–2% w.o.f.

Procedure:

1. Fill a nonreactive vessel with enough warm water to allow the textile to float freely. The water should be warm enough to dissolve the iron but not hot (≈60°C/140°F).

2. Add the ferrous sulfate and sodium acetate. Stir until completely dissolved. When combined they form ferrous acetate.

3. Place the dyed, wetted-out textile into the bath. Do not heat. Watch the textile carefully and remove it when the desired color is reached, keeping in mind that textiles always dry to a lighter shade than when wet. The iron attaches quickly and should take no longer than a few minutes.

4. Rinse and then wash the textile thoroughly to remove any unattached iron.

5. After using the dye vessel, scour it thoroughly to remove any iron residue.

RECIPE 15

POST-MORDANTING WITH IRON OR COPPER FROM EITHER A DYE VESSEL OR METAL SCRAPS (FOR WOOL OR CELLULOSE)

Iron can be leached from an iron pot, and copper may be obtained from a copper or brass pot. If such a pot is not available, pieces of iron or copper pipe can be incorporated in a stainless steel vessel. Place these metal pieces underneath a rack or shelf in the pot to prevent damage to the textile. The extraction of metal is most successful when the liquid bath is slightly acidified. Use alum to acidify the bath. Avoid citric acid or cream of tartar because they can have a detrimental effect on the aluminum mordant bond. The advantage of this approach is that the textile absorbs all iron or copper extracted from the metal, and there is no residual metal remaining in the water.

Procedure:

1. Add water and a small amount of alum (just enough alum to acidify the bath to pH 3.5–4.0).

2. Place the dyed, wetted-out textile into the bath.

3. Heat the bath gently to a near simmer (≈90°C/195°F). Watch the textile carefully and remove it when the desired color is reached.

4. Rinse and then wash the textile thoroughly to remove any unattached iron.

NOTE: Pre-mordanting of the textile may also be done in an iron or copper vessel; this will attach either alum and iron or alum and copper at the same time, depending on the pot selected. Results obtained from using this method might not be consistent or repeatable, which is especially important to consider when doing production dyeing or when working with large quantities of dyes and textiles.

Recycling a Dye Bath

RECIPE 16

. . . .

TO MAKE A DYE LAKE FROM A LEFTOVER DYE BATH

Ingredients:

- Alum at 10 g/L (volume to be determined)

- Soda ash at 5 g/L (volume to be determined)

Procedure:

1. Strain out any solid dye plant materials that might be in the dye bath. Estimate the amount of liquid (in liters) remaining in the bath. Be sure that the bath is in a vessel with plenty of extra space to accommodate a large amount of bubbling that will take place when the solution is neutralized. A tall, narrow vessel is ideal.

2. Weigh the alum at 10 g/L of liquid volume.

3. Slowly add the alum directly to the dye bath if it is still warm. If the bath has cooled, dissolve the alum in a small amount of hot water before adding to the bath. Stir gently. The alum will bind with some of the remaining dye, turning it into a pigment. Careful observations will reveal small particles of dye pigment suspended in the solution. The solution will be slightly acidic, and the process is not complete until the bath has been neutralized.

4. Weigh soda ash (sodium carbonate) at 5 g/L of liquid volume.

5. Either slowly add the soda ash directly to the warm bath or dissolve the soda ash in a small amount of hot water before adding it to the bath. The soda ash will neutralize the acid of the alum and will cause the solution to bubble dramatically. The reaction that results from combining a weak acid with an alkali is harmless. Keep stirring the solution until the bubbles dissipate. Test the pH, which should be neutral (pH 7). Adjust as necessary. The soda ash causes the dye pigment to form in the bath and to precipitate. It will sink to the bottom of the vessel and separate from the water.

6. Allow the bath to sit, undisturbed, for an hour or more. As the lake pigment settles to the bottom, the liquid on top will become nearly clear. Carefully pour off some of the clear liquid and discard it. Stop pouring off the clear liquid before the settled lake pigment is disturbed.

7. Strain the remaining lake pigment solution through a medium-density cotton cloth, such as a flannel. The best method is to wet out the straining cloth and use the wet cloth to line a colander or sieve that has been placed over an empty vessel. Pour the lake pigment solution into the strainer. Only the water should flow through. Initially, a small amount of the dye pigment can pass through the strainer before the holes in the straining cloth fill up with the pigment. Pour that colored liquid back through the strainer again. Once the liquid has been eliminated, the lake pigment will be the consistency of a thick pudding.

8. Store the pigment in a tightly covered jar at room temperature. Add a few drops of clove oil, or another essential oil, to the lake pigment to prevent bacteria from growing. The lake pigment will keep for many months at room temperature. It can be used for split-lake dyeing (recipe 18) or pigment application.

Refer to recipe 31.

Chapter 11

Recipes

RECIPE 17

....

A ONE-BATH ACID DYE FOR PROTEIN FIBERS

Ingredients:

- Selected dye (extract or plant material)

- Citric acid at 10% w.o.f. or enough vinegar to cause the solution to reach pH 3.5–4.0

- Tannin (gallnut tannin or other gallic or ellagic tannin or tannic acid) at 10% w.o.f.

Procedure:

1. Prepare the dye bath by extracting dye source material or dissolving the dye extract, using enough warm water to float the textile freely.

2. Add the tannin and acid to the dye bath. Stir to dissolve/distribute. Check that the pH has reached 3.5–4.0.

3. Place the wetted-out textile into the bath.

4. Slowly increase the temperature of the dye bath to ≈90°C/195°F and maintain it at that temperature for approximately 1 hour. Move the textile in the bath frequently.

5. If using vinegar, periodically check the pH during the dyeing, since the acetic acid can evaporate. Adjust as necessary.

6. Allow the textile to cool in the bath.

7. Rinse the textile in warm water. Washing at high temperatures can break the bond between the fiber and the dye, causing some of the dye to be released from the fiber into the water bath.

8. Dry the textile.

RECICE 18

....

DYEING BY USING SPLIT DYE LAKES

Dyeing with split lake-pigments is only recommended for wool. No mordant application is required prior to dyeing.

Ingredients:
- A dye lake (recycled from a dye bath)
- Citric acid

Procedure:

1. Fill a nonreactive pot with enough warm water to allow the textile to float freely.

2. Add the dye lake. Quantities may vary depending on available pigment and its strength. Stir the pigment so that there are no lumps in the dye bath. Look at the solution very closely, and you are likely to see small particles of undissolved pigment suspended in the bath.

3. Add a small amount of citric acid and stir to dissolve. Continue to add citric acid until the pH of the solution indicates 3.5. When the bath reaches this level of acidity, the dye lake will split (the mordant and dye separate) and the dye once again becomes soluble.

4. Place the wetted-out wool textile into the bath.

5. Slowly heat the dye bath to ≈90°C/195°F (just below a simmer). Maintain this temperature for approximately 1 hour. The dye and some of the mordant will penetrate into the wool fiber. The high acidity of the bath prevents the dye lake from re-forming in the liquid bath.

6. Allow the textile to cool in the bath.

7. Remove the textile from the bath; squeeze out the excess dye and immediately place the textile in a mild chalk solution (10 g calcium carbonate per 1 L water). The mild alkalinity of the chalk will encourage the lake to re-form inside the fiber.

8. A post-treatment, using a room-temperature mordant bath, will further ensure that a dye lake is formed inside the fiber.

9. Rinse the textile and then wash thoroughly.

Recipes

The Organic Indigo Vats

Refer to chapter 6 both for specific details and general instructions for preparing all vats, including dyeing with and maintaining the vats.

RECIPE 19

. . . .

THE SUGAR VAT

Of all the organic indigo vats, this is the quickest vat to get started, and it requires no cooking of the sugar. It is an excellent vat for testing, but it is not the best choice for long-term use. All ingredients are measured by weight.

Ingredients:

- 1 part indigo (2–10 g/L)
- 2 parts alkali: lime/calcium hydroxide (4–20 g/L)
- 3 parts reduction material / sugar (6–30 g/L)

The sugar for this vat must be a fruit sugar such as fructose, honey, date sugar, or glucose. Table (cane or beet) sugar will not reduce the vat.

Procedure:

1. Heat approximately half of the water required for vat to a temperature near boiling.

2. Pour the hot water into the dye vessel.

3. Dissolve the sugar in boiling water and stir it carefully into the vat.

4. Add the prepared indigo pigment.

5. Add the lime.

6. Add additional warm water to reach the desired volume.

7. Stir the vat carefully, using a centrifugal motion. Cover. Stir the vat an additional two or three times over the next few hours to activate all the ingredients.

RECIPE 20

....

THE FRUIT VAT (INCLUDES RIPE FRUIT, VEGETABLES, OR FRUIT PECTINS)

Use a reduction material that is available and inexpensive. Refer to chapter 6 for suggested fruits or vegetables that can be used as reduction materials.

Ingredients:
- 1 part indigo (2–10 g/L)
- 2 parts alkali: lime / calcium hydroxide (4–20 g/L)
- Sufficient reduction material. See note below.

NOTE: The equivalent of one banana is usually enough to reduce a 1 L vat, but that will depend on the size, ripeness, and sugar content of the banana. Experiment with quantities of fruits and vegetables. If the reduction is not strong enough, additional sugar or fruit material should be added.

Procedure:
1. Cook the fruit/vegetables in water for approximately 30 to 40 minutes to extract the sugars. The material should be very soft and broken down.
2. Strain the liquid extraction to remove the solids. The extraction liquid is used as the base liquid for the vat.
3. Pour the extraction liquid into the dye vessel.
4. Add the prepared indigo pigment.
5. Add the lime.
6. Add additional warm water to reach the desired volume.
7. Stir the vat carefully, using a centrifugal motion. Cover. Stir the vat an additional two or three times over the next few hours to activate all the ingredients.

NOTE: Extraction liquid from fruit can be used to "feed" a fructose or plant indigo vat.

RECIPE 21

....

THE PLANT VAT (HENNA, MADDER, RHUBARB ROOT)

NOTE: The complex sugars from these plants make them a good choice for vats that will be maintained for a long period of time. The plant material may be used as a dye prior to making the indigo vat.

Ingredients:

- 1 part indigo (2–10 g/L)
- 2 parts alkali: lime/calcium hydroxide (4–20 g/L)
- 3 parts finely ground reduction plant material (6–30 g/L)

Procedure:

1. Cook the finely ground plant material in boiling water (30–40 minutes). If the plant material has been used for dyeing, use the "exhausted" dye extraction to make the vat.

2. Strain the solids from the liquid extraction. The extraction liquid is used as the base liquid for the vat. If the plant particles are very fine, they can be included in the vat. Sugars will continue to be extracted from these materials.

3. Pour the extraction liquid into the dye vessel.

4. Add the prepared indigo pigment.

5. Add the lime.

6. Add additional warm water to reach the desired volume.

7. Stir the vat carefully, using a centrifugal motion. Cover. Stir the vat an additional two or three times over the next few hours to activate all the ingredients.

8. The vat can be fed by using sugars, additional plant extractions, or cooked fruit extractions.

RECIPE 22

....

THE IRON (MINERAL) VAT

The amount of alkaline material required in this vat is greater than for the sugar and plant vats. Because of the high alkalinity of this vat, it is only suitable for dyeing cellulose fibers. The vat will begin with a pH of 12–13 and will remain near a pH of 12.

Ingredients:

- 1 part indigo (2–10 g/L)
- 2 parts ferrous sulfate
- 3 parts alkali: lime (calcium hydroxide)

Procedure:

1. Fill the vessel about ¾ full with very hot water.

2. Add the hydrated indigo, the ferrous sulfate, and the lime.

3. Add additional hot water to reach the desired volume.

4. Stir the vat carefully, using a centrifugal motion. Cover. Stir the vat an additional two or three times over the next few hours to activate all the ingredients.

5. Full reduction of the iron vat will usually take 2–3 days. Once reduced, the liquid below the surface the vat should be a clear yellow or bronze color.

6. The iron vat will precipitate a plaster-like sludge, creating more sediment than the other vats. The vat does not need regular "feeding" like the sugar and plant vats do. If the vat becomes weak and requires additional indigo, it is best to make a small, concentrated "mother vat," using all the original ingredients in the same proportion. A portion of the concentrated mother vat can be used to feed the working vat, boosting both the amount of indigo and the reduction. When the sediment becomes deep, leaving little space for dyeing, discard it and make a new vat.

Refer to recipe 11 for information about dyeing and maintaining all the organic indigo vats.

PROPORTIONS OF INGREDIENTS FOR THE INDIGO VAT REDUCED WITH SUGARS, FRUIT, OR PLANTS

Sugar, Fruit, or Plant Vat			Ideal pH: 10-11
	Weak vat g/liter	Medium vat g/liter	Strong vat g/liter
1 part indigo	2 g	5 g	8 g
2 parts lime	4 g	10 g	16 g
3 parts reduction material	6 g	15 g	24 g

PROPORTIONS OF INGREDIENTS FOR THE INDIGO VAT REDUCED WITH IRON

Iron Vat			Ideal pH: 12
	Weak vat g/liter	Medium vat g/liter	Strong vat g/liter
1 part indigo	2 g	5 g	8 g
2 parts ferrous sulfate	4 g	10 g	16 g
3 parts lime	6 g	15 g	24 g

Recipes

Printing Recipes

GUM THICKENERS

When using guar gum as a thickening agent in any of these recipes, add only a small amount at a time, stirring constantly. Use a small mixer or handheld blender, if possible, to distribute the gum evenly. Guar gum thickens as it absorbs liquid. Once the gum is incorporated, allow the solution to sit for about 30 minutes before using, to ensure that the gum is fully hydrated. The amount of gum can be increased, if necessary, for some applications. Gum tragacanth can be substituted for guar gum at 1.5 g per 100 g of solution in any of the following recipes.

MORDANTS FOR PRINTING ON CELLULOSE

 NOTE: Acetate mordants for printing will keep for only a couple days and must be kept cool and covered.

Aluminum acetate is a colorless mordant and difficult to see when applied to the textile. The mordant can be made visible by adding a very small amount of dissolved brazilwood extract. Add just enough to turn the solution a pale pink color so that it can be seen when applied. This will not interfere with any subsequent dye application.

Three **aluminum acetate recipes for printing** are included. Two **ferrous acetate recipes** are included. They are equally effective when applied to the textile. Choose a recipe based on available ingredients.

RECIPE 23A

ALUMINUM ACETATE FOR PRINTING (NEUTRAL ALUMINUM TRIACETATE)

Ingredients:

Alum	12 g
Sodium acetate	10 g
Guar gum	1 g
Warm water	77 g
Total	100 g

Procedure:

1. Dissolve the alum completely in the warm water.

2. Add the sodium acetate and stir to dissolve.

3. Add the gum, while stirring.

RECIPE 23B
. . . .

ALUMINUM ACETATE FOR PRINTING (NEUTRAL ALUMINUM TRIACETATE)

Ingredients:

Alum	10 g
Soda ash	5 g
Vinegar (5% acetic acid)	84 g
Guar gum	1 g
Total	100 g

Procedure:

1. Dissolve the alum and soda ash in vinegar. Stir. The solution will bubble. Be sure to use a large enough container to contain the bubbles. Continue to stir until the bubbles dissipate.

2. Add the gum, while stirring.

RECIPE 23C
. . . .

DIBASIC OR MONOBASIC ALUMINUM ACETATE FOR PRINTING

Ingredients:

Dibasic or monobasic aluminum acetate powder	5 g
Water	94 g
Guar gum	1 g
Total	100 g

Chapter 11
Recipes

Procedure:

1. Dissolve monobasic or dibasic aluminum acetate completely in warm water.

2. Add the gum, while stirring.

RECIPE 24A

FERROUS ACETATE FOR PRINTING

Ingredients:

Ferrous sulfate	2 g
Sodium acetate	2 g
Water	95 g
Guar gum	1 g
Total	100 g

Procedure:

1. Dissolve the ferrous sulfate completely in warm water.

2. Add the sodium acetate and stir to dissolve.

3. Add the gum, while stirring.

This version of ferrous acetate can be diluted with water to make a weaker mordant.

RECIPE 24B

FERROUS ACETATE FOR PRINTING

Ingredients:

Ferrous sulfate	4 g
Soda ash	2 g
Vinegar	93 g
Guar gum	1 g
Total	100 g

Procedure:

1. Dissolve the ferrous sulfate completely in warm water.

2. Add the vinegar and stir to dissolve.

3. Add the gum, while stirring.

This version of ferrous acetate can be diluted with vinegar to make a weaker mordant.

Quick Comparison of Mordant Recipes for Printing

COMPARISON OF ALUMINUM ACETATE RECIPES FOR MORDANT PRINTING

Aluminum Acetates

Recipe	Dibasic or monobasic Aluminum acetate	Alum	Sodium acetate	Soda ash	Liquid
23A		12%	10%		Water
23B		10%		5%	Vinegar
23C	5%				Water

COMPARISON OF FERROUS ACETATE RECIPES FOR MORDANT PRINTING

Ferrous Acetates

Recipe	Ferrous sulfate	Sodium acetate	Soda ash	Liquid
23A	4%	4%		Water
23B	4%		2%	Vinegar

149

Recipes

Mixing Mordants for Shading Effects

Aluminum acetate and ferrous acetate mordants can be mixed in combination. Either mordant can also be diluted for lighter shades. Mix the mordants either before or after adding the gum. Always apply each mordant by using a separate brush or applicator to avoid contamination.

The following chart is our recommended approach to achieve six different mordants for shading effects. Determine the quantities of mordants needed. Mix full-strength aluminum acetate and ferrous acetate mordants. If necessary, thicken the mordants with guar gum. Measure the thickened mordants by weight for greatest accuracy.

SUGGESTED PROPORTIONS FOR MIXING ALUMINUM ACETATE AND FERROUS ACETATE MORDANTS FOR PRINTING

MORDANT	Full Strength Aluminum Acetate (thickened with 1% guar)	Full Strength Ferrous Acetate (Thickened with 1% guar)	Water or vinegar (Thickened with 1% guar)
#1 Weak aluminum acetate	25%		75%
#2 Full strength aluminum acetate	100%		2%
#3 Alum/ferrous acetate	75%	25%	
#4 Weak ferrous acetate		25%	75%
#5 Full strength ferrous acetate		100%	

Procedure to Apply the Mordants

Apply the mordants to a scoured, dry textile, using a brush, silkscreen, stencil, or printing block.

Once the mordants have been applied, allow them to dry completely, preferably overnight. When dry, the smell of vinegar from the acetate mordants should be gone or very weak. Use a dry iron to completely evaporate any remaining vinegar smell.

Neutralize and fix the mordants by dunging. The ferrous mordants will change to an orange rust color as they oxidize.

Rinse thoroughly.

The textile is now ready for immersion dyeing or may be dried for future dyeing.

Dunging Solutions

Soak the printed and dried textile in the dung (chalk) solution in order to neutralize and fix the mordants. Using one of the recipes below, make enough dung solution to fully immerse the textile. Soak the dry, mordanted textile in the dung solution for at least 10 minutes. Dense textiles will likely require longer soak times. Fabrics that have been tied for *shibori* may require additional soaking time to ensure they are completely wetted out. Rinse well. Proceed to dyeing, ensuring that the textile is thoroughly wetted out in the dunging solution or in a subsequent warm water bath before dyeing.

RECIPE 25A

. . . .

DUNGING SOLUTION, CHALK

Add 10 g (approximately 1 tablespoon) of chalk (calcium carbonate) per L of hot water. Stir in well.

The chalk solution can be used multiple times. The chalk will settle and only needs to be stirred up. The solution will eventually become dirty looking and, once contaminated with iron, should be discarded.

RECIPE 25B

. . . .

DUNGING SOLUTION, CHALK, AND WHEAT BRAN

NOTE: This is the preferred recipe when using thickened mordants for printing.

1. Add 10 g of chalk (calcium carbonate) per L of hot water. Stir.

2. Add 1/2 cup of wheat bran per L of hot water.

3. Enzymes in the bran will dissolve and remove excess gum. Place the bran loosely in a net bag (such as one used for straining paint) to prevent bran particles from being deposited to the textile. Feed-grade bran is very inexpensive and available at farm supply stores.

RECIPE 26

. . . .

CITRIC-ACID DISCHARGE SOLUTION

This acidic paste will remove mordants from a cellulose textile.

Ingredients:

Citric acid	20 g
Water	79 g
Guar gum	1 g
Total	100 g

Procedure:

1. Prepare the textile by applying the mordant that will be discharged. Dry the mordant. If using a printing mordant, do not dung.

Recipes

2. Apply the discharge solution with a brush, stencil, printing block, or silkscreen.

3. Allow the discharge solution to dry. The dried discharge solution will be visible on the ferrous acetate mordant but may be difficult to see on the aluminum mordant.

4. Dung and rinse the textile.

5. Dry the textile if a second mordant is to be applied. Apply the additional mordant. Dry, dung, and rinse a second time.

6. Proceed to dyeing.

. . . .

NOTE: Discard the dung solution after use for discharging ferrous acetate. The dung solution will contain loose iron and will contaminate other textiles.

The discharge solution can be kept for many weeks if stored cool and covered.

Combine Dye and Mordant for Direct Application

These print pastes contain both dye and mordant with white vinegar (5% acid). There are two different approaches to mixing these pastes. Recipe 27 mixes all ingredients together in one step. This is convenient for mixing a single dye color. Recipe 28 uses a thickened paste with vinegar and mordant that is made ahead of time. This approach will simplify the mixing of several different dye extracts. When mixing these pastes, always add the alum AFTER the vinegar to ensure that the dye remains soluble.

RECIPE 27

. . . .

DYE/MORDANT PASTE FOR DIRECT APPLICATION

Ingredients:

Dye extract	1–10 g (depending on the dye)
Hot water	37–46 g
White vinegar	50 g
Alum	2 g
Guar gum	1 g
Total	100 g

Procedure:

1. Dissolve the dye extract in a small amount of the hot water.

2. After the dye extract has cooled, add the vinegar and stir well.

3. Dissolve the alum in the remaining water and add to the dye/vinegar solution. It is important to add the mordant AFTER the vinegar.

4. Add the gum while stirring.

RECIPE 28

. . . .

DYE/MORDANT PASTE WITH PREMIXED THICKENING PASTE

Step 1: Mix gum thickener with mordant and acid:

Alum	25 g
Guar gum	10 g
White vinegar	465 g
Total	500 g

Combine all ingredients. Use an electric mixer or blender to ensure that the alum and gum are well dissolved in the vinegar. The thickening paste will keep for weeks if kept cool and tightly covered.

Step 2: Dissolve the dye.

Dye extract	1–10 g (depending on the dye)
Hot water	40–49 g
Total	50 g

Step 3: Make the dye paste by mixing the dissolved dye with the acid/mordant paste.

Dissolved dye extract	50g
Acid/mordant print paste	50g
Total	100g

Recipes

Application:

1. Apply the dye mordant paste directly onto a cellulose or silk textile.

2. Allow the paste to dry completely.

3. Steam the textile for 10 to 15 minutes to ensure that the dye penetrates the fiber and the vinegar evaporates. Refer to information about steaming in the appendix.

4. Remove the textile from the steamer. Immerse the textile in a chalk bath for a few minutes to ensure that all acid has been neutralized.

5. Rinse well and boil the textile for 10 minutes in a neutral soap to finish.

These dye pastes will keep for many weeks at room temperature if tightly covered.

Suggested dye percentages for extracts:

These are suggested quantities for some dyes that are typically available as extracts. The amount of dye will depend on the depth of color desired and the strength of the dye extract. If extracts are not available, the dye paste can be made with very concentrated dye extractions. Use only a small amount of water when extracting from the dye source material. The dye pastes can be combined to mix colors or can be altered with the addition of small amounts of ferrous acetate.

Cochineal	1–2%	Lac	1–2%	Pomegranate	3–6%
Cutch	4–6%	Madder	5–10%	Weld	1–2%

Pigments and Dye Lakes (Application to Cellulose or Silk)

RECIPE 29

....

MAYA BLUE

Ingredients:

Fuller's earth clay	30 g
Indigo	3 g

Procedure:

1. Combine the indigo and clay and stir well, distributing these dry ingredients evenly.

2. Keeping the mixture dry, place it in a small, nonreactive pot and heat it slowly.

3. As the clay heats, the color will change from blue to turquoise and finally violet. The heating process takes approximately 20 minutes. Once the color becomes deep violet, sublimation will be complete, indicating that the indigo has moved into the clay.

4. Remove the Maya blue from the heat immediately and cool. As it cools, the color will return to a turquoise color.

NOTE: Any form of palygorskite, sepiolite, or attapulgite clay can be used in place of fuller's earth. Store the Maya blue in a tightly covered container. This pigment can be applied by using a binder such as soy milk.

RECIPE 30

FRESH SOY MILK

Ingredients:

Dry soybeans   25 g
Water   500 ml
plus water for pre-soaking the beans

Procedure:

Cover the beans with plenty of cool water and soak overnight. The next day, strain and rinse the beans well. Add the soybeans to a blender with 500 ml fresh, cool water. Run the blender on medium speed for 5 to 7 minutes. Be sure that the blender completely pulverizes the beans. Strain and squeeze out the liquid soy milk through a muslin straining cloth.

Fresh soy milk can be kept refrigerated for 2 to 3 days. Discard after that time.

RECIPE 31

APPLICATION OF PIGMENTS TO THE TEXTILE

Step 1: Prepare the textile.

Brush the soy milk onto a clean, dry textile. Allow the textile to dry flat or on a line. Do not apply heat, which can damage the enzymes in the soy milk. Once the textile has been treated with soy milk, the pigment should be applied within a week, while the enzymes are fresh and active.

Chapter 11

Recipes

Step 2: Apply the pigment.

Combine a pigment such as ocher, indigo, Maya blue, or lake pigment with a little fresh soy milk in a small covered plastic jar. Use approximately 1 part pigment to 3 parts soy milk by volume. Add a few glass marbles to the jar and shake the pigment and milk vigorously. The marbles act like a ball mill, crushing the pigment into smaller particles and hydrating it evenly. Remove the marbles. Lake pigment particles are already very small, and they need only to be combined well with the soy milk. Add a small amount (1% or less) of guar gum to these pastes to thicken, if desired.

Apply the pigment to the soy-treated textile with a brush, roller, or printing block, or use another method.

Allow the pigment to dry on the textile for 1 to 2 weeks.

Handwash the textile carefully to remove any excess pigment and soy milk that has not been bound to the textile. The pigment application is a surface treatment, and vigorous washing may remove more pigment than desired.

Printing and Indigo

RECIPE 32

. . . .

CLAY RESIST PASTE FOR INDIGO (FOR USE ON CELLULOSE)

Ingredients:

Magnesium sulfate (Epsom salts)	10 g
Gum arabic powder	20 g
Clay (15 g bentonite, 15 g kaolin)	30 g
Warm water	100 g
Total	160 g

Mixing the paste:

1. Dissolve the magnesium sulfate in warm water.

2. Add the gum arabic. Use an electric mixer or a handheld blender, or mix by hand and allow to sit for about 30 minutes to ensure it is completely dissolved.

3. Add the clay and wait until the clay expands and the paste becomes milky in appearance. The paste should be the texture of syrup. Additional clay can be added if the paste application requires a thicker consistency.

The paste can be stored a number of days if kept cool and covered.

156

Application:

1. Apply the clay resist paste on a well-scoured, dry textile, using a stiff brush, stamp, stencil, or silkscreen. The pastes are usually applied to only one side of the textile.

2. Dry the paste completely on the textile.

3. Immerse the dry textile into the indigo vat for approximately 10 minutes.

4. DO NOT RINSE if additional indigo dips will be done. Allow the textile and paste to dry completely before dyeing again. Continue with additional dips, without rinsing, until the desired shade is reached. The paste will hold up relatively well in the alkaline indigo vat, but it will dissolve immediately in water.

5. ALTERNATIVELY, rinse out the resist paste in water immediately after each indigo dip, and dry the textile before adding a new layer of resist. Apply the paste to different areas of the same textile to build a design that includes layers with various shades of indigo.

6. When the dyeing is complete, rinse in water to remove the paste.

7. Neutralize the indigo dyed textile by using a vinegar/water solution.

8. Boil to finish and to remove excess dye.

RECIPE 33

SOY AND LIME RESIST PASTE FOR INDIGO ON CELLULOSE

Ingredients:

Finely ground soybean powder or soy flour	20 g
Lime (calcium hydroxide)	20 g
Water, to a suitable consistency	

Procedure:

1. Mix soybean powder and lime with enough water (approximately 100 ml) to make a thin paste.

2. Apply the paste to the surface of a well-scoured, dry textile. Allow the paste to dry completely.

3. Immerse the textile in the indigo vat, using dips at least 10 minutes long. Unlike the clay paste, the soy/lime paste does not dissolve easily in water.

4. The paste can be washed off when the textile is neutralized in a vinegar rinse.

NOTE: Soy and lime resist paste can be used as a resist for the potassium permanganate indigo discharge (recipes 35 and 36).

Recipes

RECIPE 34

INDIGO PRINT PASTE FOR CELLULOSE

This paste requires multiple steps that must be followed carefully. Mix this paste a day or two before intended use, to ensure that all ingredients are completely dissolved.

CAUTION: Always wear gloves and use caution when mixing or handling this alkaline paste. Make each of these solutions in a Pyrex glass or stainless steel vessel. Once made, they can be stored in high-density polyethylene or polypropylene containers. Containers with a #2 or #5 recycling code have excellent resistance to the high alkalinity of the solution and paste.

Step 1: Lye Solution

Caustic soda (Sodium hydroxide)	125 g
Cool tap water	235 g
Lye solution	360 g

The lye solution must be made with great care! Wear protection during this process: gloves, eye or face protection, and a mask to prevent inhalation of lye vapor.

1. Measure the cold water into a Pyrex glass or stainless steel vessel. Use a nonreactive lid. to contain any fumes that might result during the mixing.

2. Place the vessel of cool tap water into a larger bath of cool tap water (forming a water jacket) and put both of these in a sink or isolated area. Mixing caustic soda with water will generate heat, and the larger cold-water bath water jacket helps keep the mixture cool.

3. Stir the caustic soda into the water a little at a time and put on the lid as a precaution to any fumes that might arise. If mixed too quickly, it will create excessive heat and fumes. This process should be done over the course of an hour or more. When mixed slowly, fumes or heat should not be a problem.

Step 2: Alkaline thickening paste

Lye solution (from step 1)	360 g
Corn dextrin	40 g
Corn starch	25 g
Total	425 g

1. Combine the corn dextrin and cornstarch. Slowly sift these dry ingredients into the lye through a fine sieve while gently, but constantly, stirring. Use gloves and eye protection. If solid particles result, allow the solution to sit for a day or two until they completely dissolve.

2. Immerse the Pyrex or stainless steel vessel (containing the lye, corn dextrin, and corn starch) in a hot water bath. Very gently heat the bath while carefully stirring, until the temperature of the lye mixture reaches 60°C/140°F. At this temperature the starch with thicken.

3. Allow the solution to cool. If additional thickening is required, add a small amount of guar gum, while slowly and carefully stirring.

NOTE: The alkaline thickening paste can be used as a clear discharge for mordant dyes. Follow the same printing process as below, leaving out the sugar solution, which is not necessary, for a clear discharge.

Step 3: Indigo solution

Indigo powder	15 g
Gum arabic powder	3 g
Water	57 g
Total	75 g

1. Place the indigo powder and gum arabic into a small plastic jar with a few glass marbles. Add the water.

2. Cover and shake vigorously to hydrate and grind the indigo and gum.

Step 4: Dark blue indigo print paste

Indigo solution	75 g
Alkaline thickening	425 g
Total	500 g

1. Combine alkaline thickening and indigo solution.

2. If a lighter color is desired, add less of the indigo solution.

The indigo print paste will keep for many months if sealed tightly.

Recipes

Step 5: Sugar Solution

Fructose	125 g
Water	375 g
Total	500 g

1. Apply sugar solution to the cellulose textile using a brush.

2. Hang the textile to dry or stretch it on a plastic-topped print table to dry flat without wrinkles. Once the sugar is dry, the textile can be stored carefully in an airtight container and printed at a later date.

Step 6: The Printing Process

1. Apply the sugar solution to the textile and dry.

2. While wearing rubber gloves, apply the dark blue indigo print paste, in a thin layer, onto the textile with a brush, stencil, or silkscreen. Be sure that the paste is thoroughly stirred, as the indigo will settle at the bottom. Clean screens and brushes carefully and as soon as possible with warm water. The alkaline paste might damage the emulsion on the screen. Use only synthetic brushes, since the high alkalinity of the paste will destroy natural bristles.

3. Dry the printed textile on a line.

4. As soon as the paste is dry (it may still be a little tacky), wrap and steam the entire textile for 10 to 15 minutes in a horizontal stovetop steamer or a steam pot (refer to steaming in the appendix, page 167). During the steaming process the alkaline indigo paste will reduce when it comes in contact with the sugared textile, resulting in a blue indigo print. A stovetop steamer is required to produce the amount of heat required to reduce the indigo. A bullet steamer does not produce adequate heat.

5. Remove the textile from the steamer and unwrap carefully. The printed indigo will appear dark and burnt looking. At this point, the indigo paste is still soluble, and care needs to be taken not to rub it on the textile. Oxidize the textile by allowing it to hang or sit flat for about 10 minutes.

6. Immerse the textile in a bath of cold water. It should be placed in a single layer so it does not fold back on itself. Leave the textile undisturbed until the color turns blue. It is then safe to wash the textile more aggressively to remove the excess paste.

7. Neutralize the textile in a vinegar solution.

8. Boil the indigo print to finish.

RECIPE 35

....

DISCHARGE OF INDIGO WITH POTASSIUM PERMANGANATE
(FOR CELLULOSE FIBERS OR SILK)

Mix the potassium permanganate discharge and citric-acid solutions separately. Create an appropriate liquid volume of each to completely immerse the textile to be discharged.

Discharge Bath: 2 g/L Potassium Permanganate Solution:

Potassium permanganate (KMnO4)	2 g
Hot tap water	enough to reach total volume
Total:	1000 ml

40 g/L Citric-Acid Solution:

Citric acid	40 g
Water	enough to reach total volume
Total	1000 ml

1. Immerse the indigo-dyed textile to be discharged into the permanganate solution. The color of the textile will go from blue to purple and finally to brown.

2. Once the textile appears brown (this may take about 5 minutes), remove it from the discharge solution, rinse lightly, and immediately immerse the textile in a 4 percent citric-acid solution. Leave it in the acid solution until all the brown has disappeared and the textile is white (or light blue). This usually takes 5–10 minutes.

3. Steps 1 and 2 can be repeated for further discharge.

4. Once the discharge is complete, neutralize the textile in a chalk/dung bath and rinse/wash well. The chalk step is very important to neutralize any remaining citric acid. The final discharge color may a very light blue or white, depending on the textile itself.

5. Finish the textile by soaking in a vinegar solution (approximately 15 ml/L of cold water).

6. Clean the textile by boiling in a neutral detergent.

The potassium solution is active for about 1 hour and will begin to deteriorate after that time. Mix only the quantity necessary and discard after use. The potassium permanganate is a very dilute solution. Manganese exists in nature and is no more harmful than iron. The citric-acid solution does not deteriorate and can be stored covered, at room temperature.

Recipes

RECIPE 36

DISCHARGE OF INDIGO WITH POTASSIUM PERMANGANATE BROWN
(ONLY FOR CELLULOSE FIBERS)

1. Mix the same potassium permanganate solution from recipe 34.

2. Mix a 50 g/L sugar solution with enough volume to immerse the textile.

Fructose (or other reducing sugar)	50 g
Warm water	enough to reach total volume
Total	1000 ml

1. Prepare the indigo-dyed textile for discharge by neutralizing it in a vinegar solution.

2. Rinse.

3. Immerse the indigo-dyed textile into the permanganate solution. The color of the textile will go from blue to purple and finally to brown.

4. Once the textile appears brown (this may take about 5 minutes), remove it from the discharge solution.

5. Immediately immerse the textile into the sugar solution. The sugar stops the oxidizing effect of the potassium permanganate. A light brown color results from the manganese dioxide. Repeat the process for deeper colors.

6. Finish the textile by soaking in a vinegar solution (approximately 15 ml/L of cold water.

7. Clean the textile by boiling in a neutral detergent.

NOTE: For a deeper brown color, treat the textile with tannin either prior to immersion in the potassium permanganate or afterwards. To obtain all three colors (blue, brown, and white) in the same textile, shift the resists (such as shibori) between applications of the permanganate/acid and permanganate/sugar. It is very important to neutralize any citric acid thoroughly before immersing the textile again in the permanganate. If acid remains in the textile, it will deteriorate the brown color.

Resist the Discharge of Indigo with a Soy/Lime Paste

1. Mix the soy/lime indigo paste (recipe 33).

2. Apply the paste to a textile that has been dyed with indigo.

3. Allow the paste to dry.

4. Immerse the pasted textile into the potassium permanganate solution prepared in recipe 35. The paste will resist the discharge solution.

5. Finish by immersing in citric-acid solution (recipe 35) or a sugar solution (recipe 36).

6. Once immersed in citric acid or a weak vinegar solution, the paste can be cleaned from the textile.

Appendix

Molecular Weights

Molecular weights are used in chemistry for calculating proportions between different chemical compounds. They are introduced here because they can be useful when compounds other than those in the recipes must be used.

Example 1: The recipe asks for alum (molecular weight of 474), and the only thing at hand is aluminum sulfate (molecular weight of 666). As you can see in the formula, there is only one aluminum atom in alum, and two in aluminum sulfate. In order to find the proportion between them, the molecular weight of alum has to be multiplied by two so that the comparable weight is 948. The two contain different amounts of aluminum per weight unit, aluminum being here the important part of the compound. The question is "How much aluminum sulfate should be used?"

If recipe asks for 100 g of alum the corresponding weight of aluminum sulfate would be:

100 g multiplied by 666 and divided by 948 = 70.25 g

Example 2: This explains the differing amounts of aluminum triacetate and dibasic aluminum acetate in recipes 11A and 11C. Dibasic aluminum acetate is stronger (molecular weight of 120) than aluminum triacetate or neutral aluminum acetate (molecular weight of 204).

Recipe 11A asks for 8 percent of the weight of textile of neutral aluminum acetate. If dibasic aluminum acetate is used instead, the amount should be:

8 multiplied by 120 and divided by 204 = 4.7% of the material weight. Recipe 11C calls for a little more than half the amount as in the recipe 11A.

The following table contains most of the compounds used in the recipes in this book. All the weights are based on oxygen having the atomic weight of 16 and without many decimals, which is precise enough for our purposes.

The Function and Use of the Hydrometer

An instrument called a hydrometer has been used for centuries in textile production to measure and control the strength of chemical solutions efficiently. A hydrometer is normally made of glass. It is a cylindrical stem and bulb, with weight in the bulb to make it float upright.

The hydrometer is used to measure the specific gravity or chemical density of a liquid solution. A sample to be measured is placed in a deep, narrow vessel, and the hydrometer is carefully lowered into the solution (using a slight rotation). When the instrument

again becomes steady, the specific gravity of that particular solution can be determined from the numbers on the side of the glass tube.

There are two historical systems of measurement of specific gravity (the Twaddle system and "degrees Baumé"). The most commonly used measurement system today is in "degrees Baumé."

Hydrometers are sold for narrow ranges of specific gravity, so a user must know the approximate range of density or specific gravity that will be measured. Additionally, the instruments are designed for use in

MOLECULAR WEIGHTS OF CHEMICALS USED COMMONLY FOR DYEING

Name	Formula	Weight
Acetic acid	$C_2H_4O_2$	60
Alcohol	C_2H_5OH	46
Alum (potassium)	$Al\ K(SO_4)_2 + 12H_2O$	474
Aluminum acetate	$Al(C_2H_3O_2)_3$	204
Aluminum acetate dibasic	$Al(OH)_2(C_2H_3O_3)$	120
Aluminum acetate monobasic	$Al(OH)(C_2H_3O_3)_2$	162
Aluminum hydroxide	$Al_2(OH)_6$	156
Aluminum sulfate	$Al_2(SO_4)_3 + 18H_2O$	666
Ammonia	NH_3	17
Ammonium acetate	$NH_4C_2H_3O_2$	77
Ammonium hydroxide	NH_4OH	35
Calcium acetate	$Ca(C_2H_3O_2)_2$	158
Calcium oxide	CaO	56
Caustic potash	KOH	56
Caustic soda	$NaOH$	40
Chalk	$CaCO_3$	100
Citric acid	$(HOOCCH_2)_2C(OH)(COOH)$	192
Epsom salt	$MgSO_4 + 7H_2O$	247
Ferrous acetate	$Fe(C_2H_3O_2)_2$	174
Ferrous sulfate	$FeSO_4 + 7H_2O$	278
Fructose	$C_6H_{12}O6$	180
Glauber's salt (cryst.)	$Na_2SO_4 + 10H_2O$	322
Glucose	$C_6H_{12}O6$	180
Glycerine	$C_3H_5(OH)_3$	92
Lactic acid	$C_3H_6O_3$	90
Lime	$Ca(OH)_2$	74
Oxalic acid	$C_2O_4H_2 + 2H_2O$	126
Potash (potassium carbonate)	$K_2CO_3 + 2H_2O$	174
Potassium permanganate	$KMnO_4$	158
Soda ash	Na_2CO_3	106
Sodium acetate	$NaC_2H_3O_2 + 3H_2O$	136
Sodium chloride	$NaCl$	59
Sodiumhydrosulphite (cryst.)	$Na_2S_2O_4 + 2H_2O$	210
Stearic acid	$C_{18}H_{36}O_2$	284
Tannin (tannic acid)	$C_{14}H_{10}O_9$	322
Tartaric acid	$C_4H_6O_6$	150
Water	H_2O	18

Appendix

narrow temperature ranges, so the user must consider that when making measurements.

If you work at a fairly constant ambient temperature, the hydrometer can still be used as a relative measure of the concentration, which makes it possible to repeat a process accurately. If the user records the specific gravity of each solution, the subsequent solutions can be adjusted to that gravity by the addition of small amounts of water or chemical.

The hydrometer can, for example, be used to test how much mordant or tannin is left in the liquid after immersion of the first lot. Both these processes leave a part of the chemical in the liquid. The remainder can then be used in a controlled way for the next lot, or more water and mordant/tannin can be added to achieve the required original concentration.

There are a few charts included for some chemicals in order to show the gravity levels relevant for natural dyeing.

SPECIFIC GRAVITY OF ALUMINUM ACETATE SOLUTIONS

Aluminum Acetate Solutions at 15°C

Specific Gravity	Degrees Bé.	Aluminum acetate g/l
1.012	1.6	20
1.025	3.4	40
1.038	5.0	60
1.050	6.7	80
1.062	8.3	100
1.074	9.9	120
1.086	11.3	140
1.098	12.8	160
1.100	13.0	163

SPECIFIC GRAVITY OF TANNIC ACID SOLUTIONS

Specific gravity	Tannic acid %
1.004	1.0
1.006	1.5
1.008	2.0
1.010	2.5
1.012	3.0
1.014	3.5
1.016	4.0
1.018	4.5
1.020	5.0
1.024	6.0
1.032	8.0
1.041	10.0
1.049	12.0
1.057	14.0
1.066	16.0
1.074	18.0
1.082	20.0

Steaming

A horizontal steamer, in which the textile can be steamed in full width, is ideal, but if it is not available, quite large pieces and samples can be steamed in a large pot. It is necessary to have a rack or grid some distance from the bottom in order to keep the textile away from the boiling water. The printed textile is packed carefully in the following way:

Both sides of the textile should be covered with an open-weave cloth such as loosely woven muslin or straining cloth. Then fold the entire packaged textile lengthwise (use accordion folds) to a width fitting into the pot, and loosely roll it into a cylinder. Place the cylinder vertically on a piece of wool felt so that the steam can pass between the layers in the roll. Cover the sides and top of the roll with pieces of wool felt. The felt prevents drops of water from falling on the textile and marring the print.

It is practical, but not necessary, to make a basket of chicken wire into which all this can be packed. Place the textile in the pot when the water is boiling and steam has begun to rise. The basket makes this safer and prevents loss of heat and steam, since it can be safely packed outside the pot and just dropped in when the water is boiling. Place the lid on the pot and begin timing. Remove the textile from the steam pot carefully to avoid being burned.

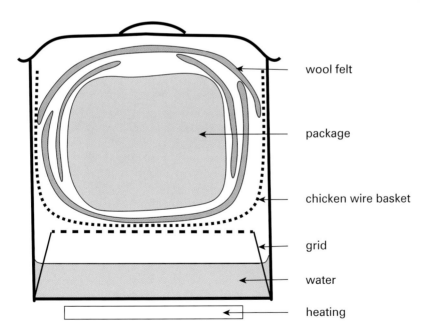

wool felt

package

chicken wire basket

grid

water

heating

Stovetop steaming: for direct printing with dye and mordant and with indigo.

Appendix

Overview of Yellow Dyes

FREQUENTLY USED FLAVONOID DYES

Common plant name(s)	Latin name	Primary flavonol
Black oak bark	*Quercus vellutina* or *Quercus tinctoria*	quercitron
Coreopsis/Tickseed	*Coreopsis tinctoria*	anthochlors
Dyer's broom/Dyer's greenwood	*Genista tinctoria*	luteolin, genistein
Golden marguerite/Dyer's chamomile	*Anthehemis tinctoria*	myrecetin, quercitron, apigenin
Goldenrod	*Solidago canadensis*	quercitron, isoquercitron, astragalin, isorhamnetin
Marigold	*Tagetes erecta* (Mexican), *Tagetes patula* (French), *Tagetes* spp.	quercetagetin, patulitrin
Old Fustic	*Maclura tinctoria*	morin
Osage orange	*Maclura pomifera*	morin
Persian berries/Dyer's buckthorn	*Rhamnus* spp.	rhamnetin
Sawwort	*Serratula tinctoria*	luteolin
Weld/Dyer's mingonette	*Reseda luteola*	luteolin, apigenin

 NOTE: Tests performed on wool would exhibit higher lightfast levels.

Lightfastness tests of flavonoid dyes on silk. Left side of each sample has been exposed.

Dyes for Mordant Printing

| MORDANTS ONLY | HENNA | MYROBALAN | POMEGRANATE | WELD |

Mordants for printing, dyed with a selection of yellow dyes.

Appendix

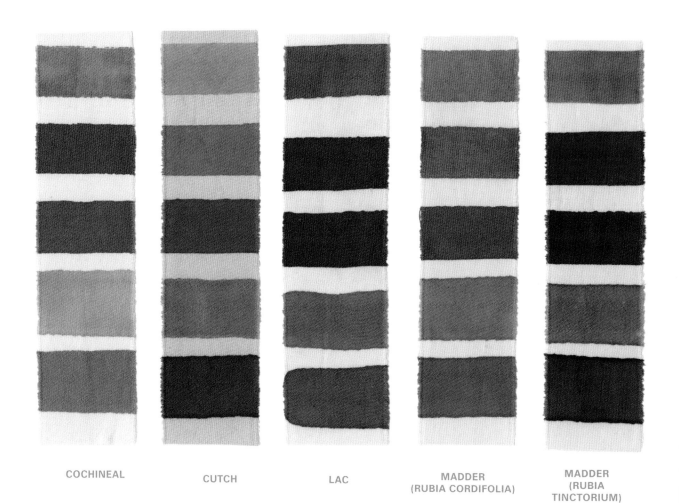

COCHINEAL   CUTCH   LAC   MADDER (RUBIA CORDIFOLIA)   MADDER (RUBIA TINCTORIUM)

Mordants for printing, dyed with a selection of
red and brown dyes.

Glossary

Acid

An acid is a chemical substance that, in solution, separates into hydrogen ions (H$^+$), and the rest of the acid is negatively charged. The higher the concentration of hydrogen ions produced by an acid, the higher its acidity and the lower the pH of the solution. For example, acetic acid, CH_3COOH, will in water separate into H$^+$ and the rest is CH_3COO^-.

The word "acid" is derived from the Latin words *acidus* or *acere*, which means "sour," since one of the characteristics of acids in water is a sour taste (e.g., vinegar or lemon juice).

Affinity

Affinity is the attraction between atoms or molecules. Affinity forces are relatively weak, and these interactions are not a result of any chemical or electronic bond.

Affinity plays a fundamental role in immersion dyeing when the dye is exhausted out of the dye bath and into the textile. We talk of dyes having high or low affinity to certain fibers. While a high affinity makes it possible to exhaust a dye bath, it is more difficult to get an even dyeing, since the dyestuff attaches too quickly. The affinity is dependent on the temperature, and many dye processes are conducted by slowly raising the temperature in order to distribute the dye properly. Influencing the positive or negative charges of the fiber by addition of acids or salts can further control dye exhaustion.

Base (alkali)

In general, a base is a substance that can accept hydrogen ions (H$^+$). In water, bases yield solutions in which the hydrogen ion activity is lower than it is in pure water; that is, the solution has a pH higher than 7.0. Most bases deliver OH$^-$ ions when in solution.

Bases can be thought of as the chemical opposite of acids. Bases and acids are seen as opposites because the effect of an acid is to increase the hydrogen ion concentration in water, whereas bases reduce this concentration. A reaction between an acid and base is called neutralization.

Carbohydrates

Carbohydrates consist of sugars and compounds built of sugars. They are present in plants and animals. These include sugars such as glucose and fructose (monosaccharides), compound sugars such as household sugar (sucrose, a disaccharide), starch, dextrins, cellulose, and pectins. Most of these will decompose by chemicals or by fermentation into fructose, glucose, or both. This is what happens in the organic indigo vats.

Detergent

A detergent is a surfactant or mixtures of surfactants with the ability to remove oils, fat, and dirt.

Dextrin

A dextrin is a decomposed starch. The starch consists of long straight and branched chains of connected glucose units that can be broken down into shorter chains by enzymes, acids, or heat. There is a wide range of dextrins with different chain lengths and different properties. Dextrin is here used as a thickening agent for printing with indigo. Dextrins are reductive due to the glucose content, which contributes to the reduction of the indigo.

Fructose

Fructose is a monosaccharide sugar ($C_6H_{12}O_6$). It is a reductive sugar and can be used as a mild reduction agent. It is present in fruits, sometimes together with glucose.

Glucose

Glucose is a monosaccharide sugar ($C_6H_{12}O_6$). It is a reductive sugar and can be used as a mild reductive agent. It is one of the most common organic compounds on earth and is produced in plants by photosynthesis from CO_2 and water. It is the unit from which starch, pectin, and cellulose are built by plants. If the plant compounds are broken down by fermentation, they produce glucose, which can be used for reduction of indigo in the vat.

Neutralization

Neutralization takes place when the aqueous solution of a base reacts with the aqueous solution of an acid to produce a solution of water and salt. The water (H_2O) is created by a combination of the hydroxyl ions (OH^-) from the base and the hydrogen ions (H^+) from the acid. The salt is the result of the remaining parts of the two solutions. It is important that either the base or the acid is weak or at least diluted when neutralization is undertaken. The neutralization develops a great deal of heat, and the liquid might get locally so hot that it boils explosively if overly concentrated solutions are used.

Oxidation (see Reduction and Oxidation)
pH

The pH indicates the concentration of hydrogen ions (H^+) and thus the acidity or alkalinity of a solution. Because the concentration in all cases is very small,

it is convenient to use the negative logarithm of the concentration; for example, pH 2 means that the concentration is $10^{-2} = 0.01$. In pure water there are small and equal amounts of hydrogen ions and hydroxyl ions (OH^-). The concentration of both is 10^{-7} (0.0000001), so that the pH of pure water is pH 7.

The scale of pH has the neutral point at pH 7 and normally ranges from pH 1 to pH 14:

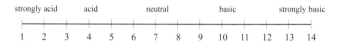

The pH can be measured by indicator strips and paper or by a pH meter. The strips are made by a finely adjusted combination of different dyes reacting to pH changes by changing color. One of these is litmus, a lichen dye, which was used alone historically to show if a solution was acidic or basic. Today several dyes are combined, making it possible to test not only acidity or basicity but also where on the pH scale it is.

pH meters measure electrically and are more accurate if calibrated properly. They must be calibrated before each use. They are more costly but make it possible to measure strongly colored liquids, which can make the strips or papers difficult to read.

Precipitation

Precipitation, in chemistry, is the process by which solid particles are separated from liquids. Some chemicals react with each other in a liquid and form insoluble substances that slowly sink to the bottom of the vessel. This is called precipitation. Precipitation takes places when cellulose fibers are mordanted. The mordant is soluble in the bath but loses its solubility during drying and settles as a solid deposit in the fibers. Another example of precipitation is the making of dye lakes. The mordant reacts with the dyes and forms insoluble compounds, called lakes, which slowly settle as a solid deposit.

Precursor

A precursor of a dye is a chemical compound that can react and form the dye. Often the real dye is not present in the plant but will be formed when the precursors are released from the plant material by either hot water or fermentation. Sometimes an oxidation takes place when the precursor is exposed to the air. For example, in the case of indigo, the precursors are different in the plants woad (*Isatis tinctoria*) and *Indigofera tinctoria*. The two plant materials are usually treated differently in order to have them produce the indigo dyestuff. Woad is composted, while *Indigofera tinctoria* is fermented and oxidized in water.

Reduction and Oxidation

There are different definitions of oxidation. Historically the word was used for the reaction with oxygen. A more general definition is that something is oxidized when it gives off electrons (e-). This is the definition used here.

Oxidation cannot take place without something else being reduced (i.e., brought to a state where it accepts electrons). The two processes are together called "redox" processes. In the indigo vat, sugars are oxidized and reduce the indigo into the soluble leuco indigo. When the leuco indigo is exposed to air, it is oxidized back into insoluble indigo.

Surfactant

Surfactants are chemical compounds that decrease the surface tension of the liquid in which they are dissolved. This is a large group of chemicals with different properties in relation to foaming, cleaning, and emulsifying. They are normally grouped into emulsifiers, wetting agents, and detergents.

Table sugar

Table sugar is a compound sugar consisting of a combination of fructose and glucose, a so-called disaccharide. It is present in sugar beets and sugar canes. While the two sugars in the compound are reductive separately, the compound is not reductive and cannot be used as a reductive agent.

Bibliography

Anon. *Manual for Printing Cotton and Other Vegetable Fibres*. Frankfurt am Main: I. G. Farben Industrie, 1936.

Anon. *Manual for the Dyeing of Cotton*. Frankfurt am Main: I. G. Farben Industrie, 1936.

Balfour-Paul, Jenny. *Indigo*. London: British Museum Press, 1998.

Böhmer, Harald. *Koekboya*. Translated by Lawrence E. Vogelberg. Ganderkesee, Germany: Remhöb Verlag, 2002.

Brunello, Franco. *The Art of Dyeing in the History of Mankind*. Translated by Bernard Hickey. Vincenza, Italy: Neri Pozza, 1973.

Cardon, Dominique. *Natural Dyes: Sources, Tradition, Technology and Science*. London: Archetype Publications, 2007.

Cardon, Dominique. *The Dyer's Handbook: Memoirs of an 18th-Century Master Colourist*. Oxford and Philadelphia: Oxbow Books, 2016.

Colby, Karen M. 1992. "A Suggested Exhibition Policy for Works of Art on Paper." *Journal of the International Institute for Conservation: Canadian Group* 17:3–11.

Galli, Andrew, dir. *Natural Dye Workshop with Michel Garcia: Colors of Provence Using Sustainable Methods*. DVD. Berkeley, CA: Slow Fiber Studios, 2011.

Galli, Andrew, dir. *Natural Dye Workshop II with Michel Garcia: Colors of the Americas on Wool Fibers Using Sustainable Methods*. DVD. Berkeley, CA: Slow Fiber Studios, 2012.

Galli, Andrew, dir. *Organic Dyes to Pigments: Foundations for the Colors of Europe*. DVD. Berkeley, CA: Slow Fiber Studios, 2014.

Gohl, Erhard, Paul Gottlieb, and L. D. Vilensky. *Textile Science*. 2nd ed. Melbourne, Australia: Longman Cheshire, 1983.

Hofenk de Graaff, Judith. *The Colourful Past*. Riggisberg, Switzerland: Abegg Stiftung, 2004.

Kirby, Jo, Maarten van Bommel, and André Verhecken, eds. *Natural Colorants for Dyeing and Lake Pigments: Practical Recipes and Their Historical Sources*. London: Archetype Books, 2014.

Knecht, Edmund, and James Best Fothergill. *The Principles and Practice of Textile Printing*. 4th ed. London: Griffin, 1952.

Kwon, Charllotte, dir. *Indigo: A World of Blue.* DVD. Vancouver, BC: Maiwa Productions, 2008.

Kwon, Charllotte, and Tim McLaughlin, dirs. *In Search of Lost Colour: The Story of Natural Dyes*. DVD. Vancouver, BC: Maiwa Productions, 2007.

Lance, Mary, dir. and prod. *Blue Alchemy: Stories of Indigo*. DVD. Corrales, NM: New Deal Films, 2011.

Liles, Jim N. *The Art and Craft of Natural Dyeing*. Knoxville: University of Tennessee Press, 1990.

Rath, Hermann. *Lehrbuch der Textilchemie*. Berlin and Heidelberg, Germany: Springer Verlag, 1972.

Rubia. DVD. Dinteloord, The Netherlands: Rubia Pigmenta Naturalia, 2006.

Schweppe, Helmut. *Handbuch der Naturfarbstoffe*. Landberg am Lech, Germany: Ecomed, 1992.

Sandberg, Gösta. *Indigo Textiles: Technique and History*. Asheville, NC: Lark, 1989.

Sundström, Carla, and Erik Sundström. *Färga med svampar*. Västerås, Sweden: ICA Bokförlag, 1982.

Turkey Red Journal. www.turkeyredjournal.com

Index

Joy Boutrup has a background in textile engineering, chemistry, and history. She has taught for many years and has a unique ability to develop new methods and techniques, based on both old and new technologies. She lives in Denmark.

Catharine Ellis is a textile artist, educator, and the author of *Woven Shibori*. Her work integrates both weaving and dyeing. She has focused her study on natural dyes for the last 10 years. She lives in the mountains of North Carolina. www.ellistextiles.com

Photos courtesy of Robin Dreyer